SCHOLASTIC

National Curriculum

Maths

Practice Book for

Year 6

Book End, Range Road, Witney, Oxfordshire, OX29 0YD
www.scholastic.co.uk

1 2 3 4 5 6 7 8 9   4 5 6 7 8 9 0 1 2 3

British Library Cataloguing-in-Publication Data
A catalogue record for this book is available from the British Library.

ISBN 978-1407-12893-1
Printed and bound in India by Replika Press Pvt. Ltd.

Editorial
Rachel Morgan, Robin Hunt, Kate Baxter, John Davis

Design
Scholastic Design Team: Neil Salt, Nicolle Thomas
and Oxford Designers & Illustrators Ltd

Cover Design
Dipa Mistry

Cover Illustration
James W Hunter

Illustration
Tomek.gr

Contents

Why buy this book?

The *100 Practice Activities* series has been designed to support the National Curriculum in schools in England. The curriculum is challenging in mathematics and includes the requirement for children's understanding to be secure before moving on. These practice books will help your child revise and practise all of the skills they will learn at school, including some topics they might not have encountered previously.

How to use this book

- The content is divided into National Curriculum topics (for example, Addition and subtraction, Fractions and so on). Find out what your child is doing in school and dip into the relevant practice activities as required. The index at the back of the book will help you to identify appropriate topics.
- Share the activities and support your child if necessary using the helpful quick tips at the top of most pages.
- Keep the working time short and come back to an activity if your child finds it too difficult. Ask your child to note any areas of difficulty at the back of the book. Don't worry if your child does not 'get' a concept first time, as children learn at different rates and content is likely to be covered throughout the school year.
- Check your child's answers using the answers section on www.scholastic.co.uk/100practice/mathsy6 where you will also find additional interactive activities for your child to play, and some extra resources to support your child's learning (such as number grids and a times tables chart).
- Give lots of encouragement and tick off the progress chart as your child completes each chapter.

How to use the book

This tells you which topic you're working on.

This is the title of the activity.

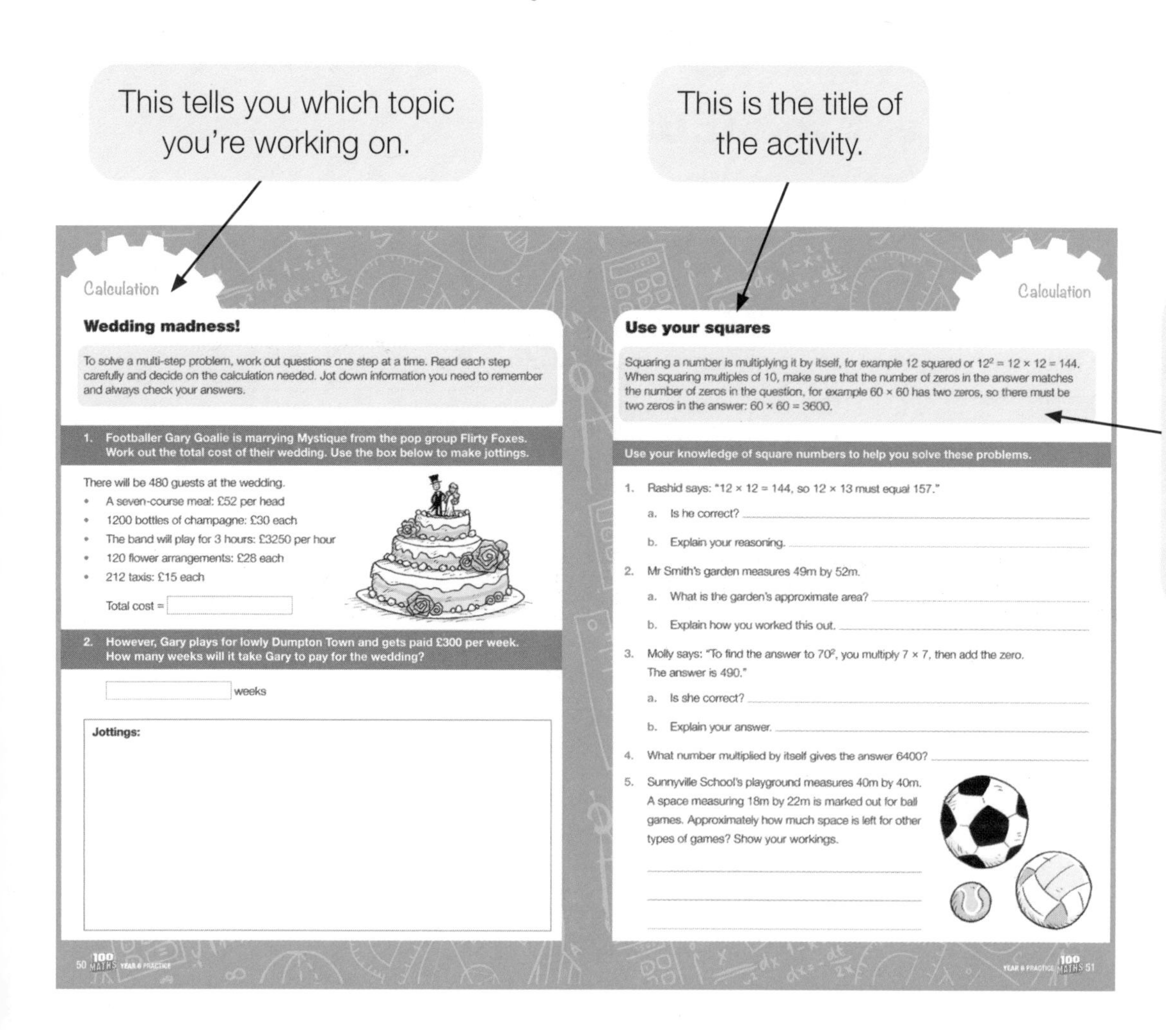

Calculation

Wedding madness!

To solve a multi-step problem, work out questions one step at a time. Read each step carefully and decide on the calculation needed. Jot down information you need to remember and always check your answers.

1. Footballer Gary Goalie is marrying Mystique from the pop group Flirty Foxes. Work out the total cost of their wedding. Use the box below to make jottings.

There will be 480 guests at the wedding.

- A seven-course meal: £52 per head
- 1200 bottles of champagne: £30 each
- The band will play for 3 hours: £3250 per hour
- 120 flower arrangements: £28 each
- 212 taxis: £15 each

Total cost =

2. However, Gary plays for lowly Dumpton Town and gets paid £300 per week. How many weeks will it take Gary to pay for the wedding?

weeks

Jottings:

50 100 MATHS YEAR 6 PRACTICE

Calculation

Use your squares

Squaring a number is multiplying it by itself, for example 12 squared or $12^2 = 12 \times 12 = 144$. When squaring multiples of 10, make sure that the number of zeros in the answer matches the number of zeros in the question, for example 60×60 has two zeros, so there must be two zeros in the answer: $60 \times 60 = 3600$.

Use your knowledge of square numbers to help you solve these problems.

1. Rashid says: "$12 \times 12 = 144$, so 12×13 must equal 157."
   a. Is he correct?
   b. Explain your reasoning.
2. Mr Smith's garden measures 49m by 52m.
   a. What is the garden's approximate area?
   b. Explain how you worked this out.
3. Molly says: "To find the answer to 70^2, you multiply 7×7, then add the zero. The answer is 490."
   a. Is she correct?
   b. Explain your answer.
4. What number multiplied by itself gives the answer 6400?
5. Sunnyville School's playground measures 40m by 40m. A space measuring 18m by 22m is marked out for ball games. Approximately how much space is left for other types of games? Show your workings.

YEAR 6 PRACTICE 100 MATHS 51

These boxes will help you with the activity. (If there's not one on your page, go back and find the last one.)

Algebra

In sequence

You may find it useful to explain the rules of a number sequence to someone verbally before writing it down.

1. Give the next four numbers in these sequences. Write the pattern used at the end.

a. 0 5 9 15 18

b. 0 2 8 10 16

c. 3 5.5 8 10.5 13

2. Write in the missing numbers in each of these sequences. Explain the rule that has been used to make the sequence.

a. $\frac{23}{8}$ ___ $\frac{27}{8}$ ___ $\frac{33}{8}$ ___ $\frac{41}{8}$

Rule:

b. 0.15 0.8 ___ 2.1 ___ ___ 4.05 ___

Rule:

3. This pattern continues in the same way. Answer the questions.

1 2 3 4 5 6 7 8 9 10

a. Which shape appears in the 28th position?

b. How many triangles will there be until you reach the number 40?

c. Explain how you found your answers.

92 100 MATHS YEAR 6 PRACTICE

Algebra

Algebra problems

Expressions can be simplified by putting the terms together, for example h + h + h can be written as 3h and 5y + 3 + 4 − 2y can be written as 3y + 7. Expressions are also a shorthand way of writing longer number statements or sentences, for example 'Five less than a mystery number' can be written as x − 5.

1. Simplify the following expressions.

a. $f + f + f + f =$

b. $5 + n + 10 =$

c. $g + 6 + g - 8 =$

d. $2h + h + 3h - h =$

e. $g + g + g + h + h + h =$

f. $3x + 2y + 2x - y =$

2. The mystery number is x. Draw a line to match each description in words with the correct expression.

The mystery number multiplied by six and added to two.	$x + 3$
Two divided by the mystery number.	$50 \div x$
Three more than the mystery number.	$6x + 2$
The mystery number added to two then multiplied by six.	x^2
The mystery number divided by two.	$x \div 50$
The mystery number divided by fifty.	$2 \div x$
Fifty divided by the mystery number.	$x \div 2$
The mystery number multiplied by itself.	$6(x + 2)$

YEAR 6 PRACTICE 100 MATHS 93

This is the instruction text. It tells you what to do.

Follow the instruction to complete the activity.

You might have to write on lines, in boxes, draw or circle things.

If you need help, ask an adult!

Read and write numbers to 10,000,000

Practise and make sure that you have a good understanding and use of six-digit numbers before going on to millions up to ten million. Continue to use abacus frameworks if you have difficulty knowing where to position zeros as place holders.

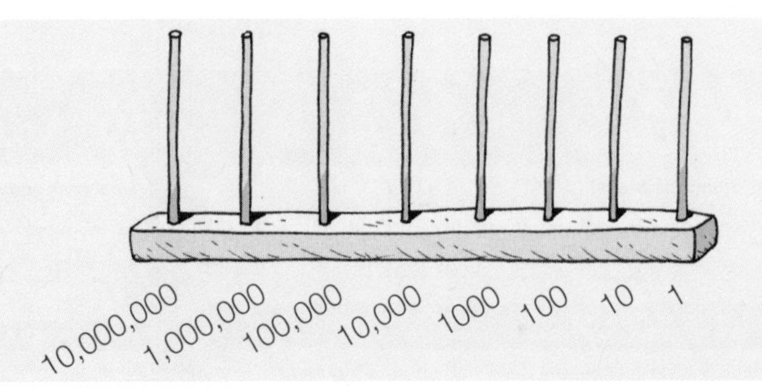

1. Write these amounts in figures.

a. six hundred and one ______________

b. four thousand and nine ______________

c. twenty thousand, six hundred and three ______________

d. one million, six hundred and twenty thousand, four hundred and ninety-one ______________

e. four hundred and seven thousand, one hundred and seven ______________

f. twenty-six thousand, three hundred ______________

g. three hundred thousand ______________

h. four thousand, nine hundred ______________

i. two million, four hundred and seven thousand, five hundred and eighty-three ______________

j. fifty-three thousand, seven hundred and twenty-four ______________

k. eighty thousand and five ______________

l. six hundred and ten ______________

m. eighty thousand, five hundred ______________

n. twenty thousand, six hundred and thirty ______________

o. four thousand and ninety ______________

2. Write these amounts in words.

a. 3020 ______

b. 8200 ______

c. 27,506 ______

d. 708,090 ______

e. 4,780,909 ______

______

3. How many:

a. thousands in 1,275,320? ______

b. hundreds in 4,008,957? ______

c. tens in 2,697,000? ______

4. Write the decimal fraction equivalent to these amounts.

a. three tenths ______

b. 5 hundredths ______

c. 12 thousandths ______

d. 8 tenths ______

e. 200 thousandths ______

f. $\frac{23}{100}$ ______

g. $\frac{4}{20}$ ______

h. forty hundredths ______

Ordering whole numbers

When ordering whole numbers it is not the size of the digits, or how many there are, but the position they are in that is important.

When using the signs < (less than) and > (greater than), it is the open part of the sign that always points towards the larger number or amount.

1. Write a number of your choice in each empty box so that the six numbers in each stack are in order.

a.	b.	c.
99,999	720,490	500,000
106,328	720,488	750,000
342,057	635,731	909,999

2. Work out these calculations and then place one of the following three signs between each pair: <, > or =.

a. $200 \div 10$ ____ 150×10

b. 25×5 ____ $135 - 39$

c. $81 \div 9$ ____ $-4 + 13$

d. $33 + 28$ ____ $87 - 26$

e. $48 \div 8$ ____ 7×8

f. 7×9 ____ $96 - 2$

3. Estimate the numbers marked by the arrows on this number line.

10,000 [ ] [ ] [ ] [ ] [ ] [ ] [ ] 9000

Rounding whole numbers

Rounding numbers helps to provide us with approximate answers. This is useful when we want to check if a calculation is likely to be correct. For example, rounding 39 × 41 to 40 × 40 = 1600 gives us a result that is close to the correct answer (1599).

1. Round these amounts to the nearest:

a. **£100**

£4251 ____________

£36,749 ____________

£843,001 ____________

£949.99 ____________

b. **1000km**

$500\frac{1}{2}$km ____________

3499km ____________

8620.3km ____________

483,995km ____________

c. **10,000 miles**

52,836 miles ____________

460,001 miles ____________

790,999 miles ____________

854,030 miles ____________

2. Round these lengths to the nearest cm.

a. 851mm ____________

b. 4439mm ____________

c. 7904mm ____________

3. Round these amounts to the nearest 1000kg.

a. 599.5kg ____________

b. 44,499kg ____________

c. 102,453kg ____________

4. Write some examples of amounts you would round to the nearest 10, 100, 1000 and 10,000, e.g. the crowd at a Grand Prix would be rounded to the nearest 1000.

a. 10 ____________

b. 100 ____________

c. 1000 ____________

d. 10,000 ____________

Positive and negative

When working with positive and negative numbers you may find it easier to put your pencil point on the number line and count the steps physically. Remember that moving in a positive direction goes to the right, and moving in a negative direction to the left.

1. Use the number line to help you solve these problems.

–10 –9 –8 –7 –6 –5 –4 –3 –2 –1 0 1 2 3 4 5 6 7 8 9 10

a. Start at –5 and jump three spaces in a positive direction. Where do you land? ____

b. Start at 4 and jump eight spaces in a negative direction. Where do you land? ____

c. Start at 9 and jump fifteen spaces in a negative direction. Where do you land? ____

d. Moving in a positive direction, give the next three numbers in this sequence.

–9 –6 –3 [ ] [ ] [ ]

e. Moving in a negative direction, give the next three numbers in this sequence.

10 6 2 [ ] [ ] [ ]

f. Put these numbers in order of size, starting with the largest.

–3 –1 4 0 6 2 ____________________

g. Put these numbers in order of size, starting with the smallest.

0 5 –4 –2 7 –8 ____________________

h. Fill in the gaps to complete this number pattern.

[ ] –5 –2 [ ] [ ] 7

Using negative numbers

1. If this fairground ride starts at –6 and moves 10 places up, where does it end?

2. Answer these questions in the same way.

a. Starts at –2 and moves 4 places down ______________

b. Starts at –9 and moves 12 places up ______________

c. Starts at 3 and moves 7 places down ______________

d. Starts at –12 and moves 5 places up ______________

e. Starts at 6 and moves 14 places down ______________

To find the difference between a positive and a negative number, add the numbers, for example the difference between –5 to +3 is 8 (5 + 3).

With two positive or two negative numbers, subtract the numbers, for example the difference between +4 to +7 is 3 (7 – 4) and the difference between –5 to –1 is 4 (5 – 1).

3. These are some of the points that the children stop at during the ride. Work out the difference between them.

a. –5 and 7 ☐ b. –12 and –6 ☐ c. 8 and –8 ☐

d. 0 and –9 ☐ e. 2 and –3 ☐ f. –4 and 11 ☐

g. 4 and 10 ☐ h. 10 and –7 ☐

4. Put the correct sign, < or >, between these pairs of positive and negative numbers.

a. –2 ☐ 1 b. 5 ☐ –5 c. 7 ☐ –9

d. 3 ☐ –4 e. 0 ☐ –2 f. –8 ☐ –10

Square number problems

A square number is a number multiplied by itself. The square of 3 is 9 because 3 × 3 = 9 and the square of 5 is 25 (5 × 5).

Try to learn all the square numbers between 1 and 100 off by heart: 1, 4, 9, 16 and so on.

1. How many squares of multiples of 10 lie between 2000 and 5000? Write as many as you can in this box. One has been done for you.

50 × 50 = 2500

2. How many squares of multiples of 10 lie between 1000 and 10,000? Write as many as you can in this box. One has been done for you.

40 × 40 = 1600

Number problems with big numbers

1000 thousand is called a million. It has six zeros: 1,000,000.
Half a million is half of 1000 thousand: 500,000. A quarter of a million is half of this: 250,000, and three quarters of a million is a half and a quarter added together:
500,000 + 250,000 = 750,000.

1. Rewrite in figures the amounts in these newspaper headlines.

a. Half a million working days lost ______________

b. £2$\frac{1}{2}$ million bingo win ______________

c. £5$\frac{1}{4}$ million spending cuts ______________

d. Massive cash robbery of £6$\frac{1}{2}$ million ______________

e. Britain has 445 million kilometres of roads ______________

2. Write in figures the number that is half a million less than the following.

a. 6 million ______________

b. 800,000 ______________

c. 7$\frac{3}{4}$ million ______________

3. Write in figures the number that is 200,000 more than the following.

a. 1 million ______________

b. 6,500,000 ______________

c. 4$\frac{1}{4}$ million ______________

4. What is the value of each circled digit?

a. 1,2(6)4,319 ______________

b. (4),375,610 ______________

c. 840,(1)23 ______________

d. 1,(2)34,567 ______________

e. 534,01(7) ______________

f. (1)0,500,000 ______________

Stadium rounding

To round to the nearest 1000, look at the number of 100s. If it is less than 5 stay with the current thousand; if it is 5 or more go on to the next thousand.

To round to the nearest 10,000 look at the number of 1000s and apply the same rule.

Here are the ground capacities of ten football teams in the English Premier League.

Club	Ground	Capacity	Nearest 1000	Nearest 10,000
Manchester Utd	Old Trafford	75,731		
Arsenal	Emirates Stadium	60,362		
Newcastle Utd	St. James Park	48,707		
Manchester City	Etihad Stadium	47,405		
Liverpool FC	Anfield	45,276		
Aston Villa	Villa Park	42,785		
Chelsea FC	Stamford Bridge	41,798		
Everton FC	Goodison Park	39,571		
Tottenham Hotspur	White Hart Lane	36,284		
West Ham Utd	Upton Park	35,016		

1. Round each of the ground capacities to the nearest 1000. Write it in the table.
2. Round each of the ground capacities to the nearest 10,000. Write it in the table.
3. Round these ground capacities to find the approximate total crowd attendance at the following stadiums, to the nearest 1000.

   Old Trafford and the Etihad Stadium ____________________

   Anfield and Stamford Bridge ____________________

   Emirates Stadium and Villa Park ____________________

   St. James Park and Old Trafford ____________________

   Goodison Park, White Hart Lane and Upton Park ____________________

Decimal rounding problems

To round a decimal to the nearest whole number, look at the digit in the first decimal place. To round a decimal to one decimal place, look at the digit in the second decimal place. If the digit is less than 5, round down; if it is 5 or more, round up.

8.1 will round to 8 10.5 will round to 11

5.13 will round to 5.1 7.49 will round to 7.5

1. These are the heights that ten kites reach during a kite-flying competition in the park. Round each height to the nearest metre. The first one has been done for you.

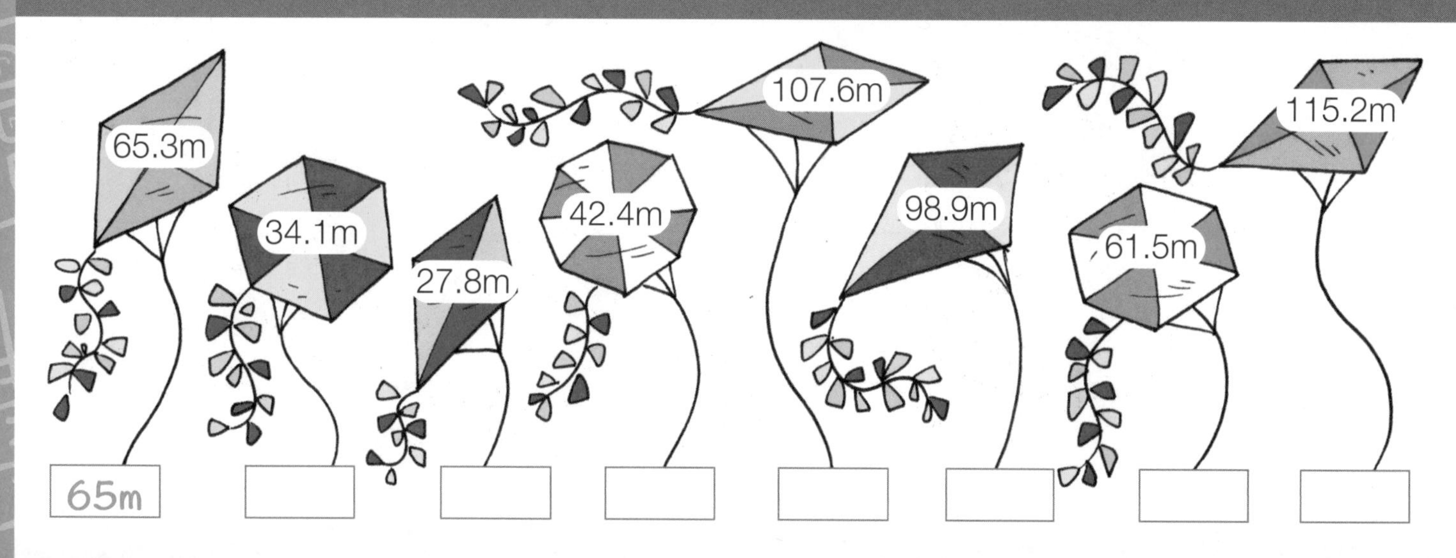

2. These distances were thrown by pupils taking part in a cricket ball-throwing competition on sports day. Round each distance to one decimal place. The first one has been done for you.

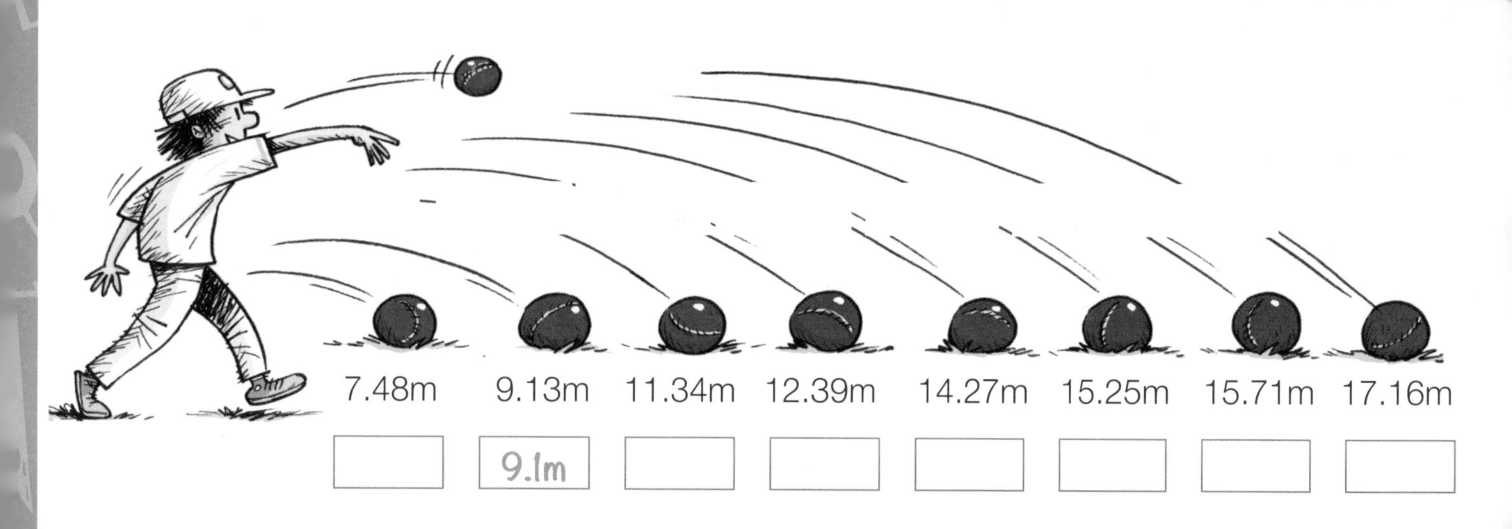

Negative number problems

Temperatures are measured in degrees, on a thermometer using the Celsius scale (°C). Numbers above zero are positive numbers (above freezing point). Numbers below zero are negative numbers (below freezing point).

1. Chilly Billy is in Iceland where the temperature is –14°C. Sunshine Sue is in Florida where the temperature is 33°C.

What is the difference between the two temperatures? ____________

2. The following week, the temperature in Iceland drops by 7°C and the temperature in Florida rises by 6°C.

What is the new temperature in Iceland? ____________

What is the new temperature in Florida? ____________

What is difference between the two temperatures? ____________

3. The coldest temperature ever recorded in Iceland is –39°C. The hottest temperature ever recorded in Florida is 43°C.

What is the difference, in degrees Celsius, between these record temperatures?

____

Bank account problems

Bank accounts with a positive number are 'in the black' or in credit. Accounts with a negative number are 'in the red' or in debit. The 'current balance' tells people how much they have in their bank account. Withdrawal means taking money out; deposit means putting money in.

1. Work out whether these children have a positive or a negative amount in their account. Tick 'in the black' for positive or 'in the red' for negative.

		In the black	In the red
a.	David earns £7.82, spends £2.19		
b.	Lucy earns £3.61, spends £5.92		
c.	Ahmed saves £8.12, spends £3.05		
d.	Ruth earns £5.80, spends £10.07		
e.	Sanjay earns £0.00, spends £5.10		
f.	Mary saves £12.00, spends £15.34		

2. Write these changes to children's bank accounts as number sentences, such as: Current balance £20, withdrawal £26 = £20 – £26 = £–6.

a. Georgia, current balance £14, withdrawal £25 = ______________________

b. Dominic, current balance £–12, deposit £18 = ______________________

c. Nina, current balance £–30, deposit £25 = ______________________

d. Marcus, current balance £50, withdrawal £35 = ______________________

e. Maria, current balance £48, withdrawal £54 = ______________________

f. David, current balance £–18, deposit £12.50 = ______________________

Fact finder

The factors of a number are the numbers that divide into it exactly.
The factors of 6, for example, are 1, 2, 3 and 6.

1. Find and list all the factors of 64. Use these factors to list as many different multiplication and division facts as you can.

$1 \times 64 = 64$

2. What about if you started with 6.4? What multiplication and division facts involving decimals can you find? Use your work in question 1 to help you.

$4 \times 1.6 = 6.4$

3. Now really challenge yourself! Start with 0.64. What facts can you find this time?

$4 \times 0.16 = 0.64$

Factors and prime numbers

A prime factor is a factor that is also a prime number. Every number can be expressed using prime factors only. For example, 18 is 6×3. This can be expressed in prime factors as $3 \times 2 \times 3$. We can then use indices to keep this simple: $18 = 3^2 \times 2$.

1. List the factors of each number. From this, can you identify the prime numbers? Circle all the prime numbers.

32	19	72	83	53
37	41	28	67	96

2. Use your knowledge of factors and prime numbers to find the prime factors of each of the numbers below. Remember, every number can be expressed using prime factors only. Look at the diagram below to help you.

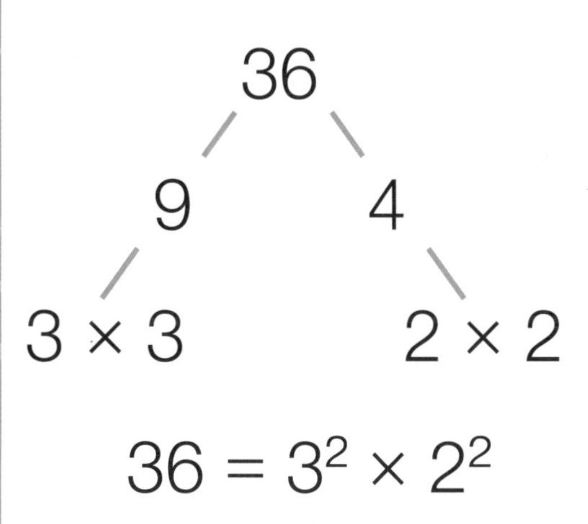

48	72
80	56

Prime factors

Prime factors can make multiplication calculations simpler. For example, 27 can expressed as 3 × 3 × 3 and 36 can be expressed as 3 × 3 × 2 × 2. So 27 × 36 can be expressed using prime factors as 3 × 3 × 3 × 3 × 3 × 2 × 2 (or $3^5 \times 2^2$) which is 972.

1. Find the prime factors of these two numbers.

24	42

2. Use these prime factors to find the answer to 24 × 42 by multiplying all the prime factors together.

3. Use prime factors to find the product of each of these pairs of numbers.

48	42	
64	28	
54	32	

Prime investigation

The number 16 has the prime factors 2 × 2 × 2 × 2.

The number 2 is the **distinct prime factor** of 16 as it is the only prime factor.

The number 14 has the prime factors 2 × 7. These are not distinct prime factors as they are different numbers.

Think about other numbers that have 2 as a distinct prime factor. How can you recognise them? What about numbers that have only a factor 3? Be confident about making predictions. It doesn't matter if your predictions are wrong – you can correct them later.

1. Use your knowledge of prime factors to work out which numbers up to 30 have just one distinct prime factor.

2. Now predict which numbers between 30 and 60 will have only one distinct prime factor. Write them in the space below.

3. Test your predictions – were you correct?

Is it correct?

Knowing multiplication facts and using tests of divisibility are good ways of checking calculations when multiplying and dividing. For all calculations, you can also use approximation and inverse calculations. Remember, addition is the inverse of subtraction, and multiplication is the inverse of division.

1. Use what you know about tests of divisibility, approximations and inverse operations to answer the questions below. Explain your reasoning each time.

a. How do you know that 714 is divisible by 6?

____

b. Is this calculation correct? 4193 × 3 = 12,478

____

c. Will says, "£20.99 × 12 is approximately £250." Do you agree?

____

d. I think of a number, add 32 and divide by 7. My answer is 6. What number did I start with?

____

e. Sally has a piece of rope 69m long. Approximately how many pieces, each measuring 4.8m, can she cut from the rope?

____

f. I think that 1032 is not divisible by 8. How can I check? Am I correct?

____

g. How can I prove that 42,768 – 31,989 = 10,779?

____

h. Prove that 1,308 ÷ 6 cannot be 219.

____

Divisibility facts

Although numbers like 2, 4, 8 and 3, 6, 9 are related to each other as a number family, they have different rules of divisibility that have to be applied to each of them separately. Once you have learned them, you can try out the rules on much larger numbers to see if they still work.

A whole number can be divided by:

- 3 if the sum of the digits is divisible by 3
- 6 if it is even and is also divisible by 3
- 8 if half of it is divisible by 4
- 9 if the sum of the digits is divisible by 9.

1. Circle the numbers in each set that can be divided exactly by 8.

a.	9	16	18	32	38	40
b.	6	22	35	48	53	62
c.	64	79	82	88	98	100

2. Circle the numbers in each set that can be divided exactly by 6.

a.	14	18	22	25	30	38
b.	12	19	24	31	36	44
c.	42	49	54	62	70	72

3. Circle the numbers in each set that can be divided exactly by 3.

a.	12	14	21	25	28	33
b.	21	29	34	36	40	48
c.	62	75	79	84	87	93

4. Circle the numbers in each set that can be divided exactly by 9.

a.	26	38	45	54	68	72
b.	105	108	144	158	172	190
c.	426	532	702	833	920	9783

Long multiplication

```
 231
 1352
×  27
27040
 9464
36504
1  1
```

In this example:

Always write the numbers in the correct columns.

Remember to add a 0 before multiplying by 2 because it is two 10s.

Carried figures should be added on to the next stage.

Both lines of working out should be totalled.

1. Use a compact written method of long multiplication to solve the following.

a. 387 × 36

b. 439 × 28

c. 1538 × 47

d. 5125 × 39

e. 5600 × 49

f. 7089 × 81

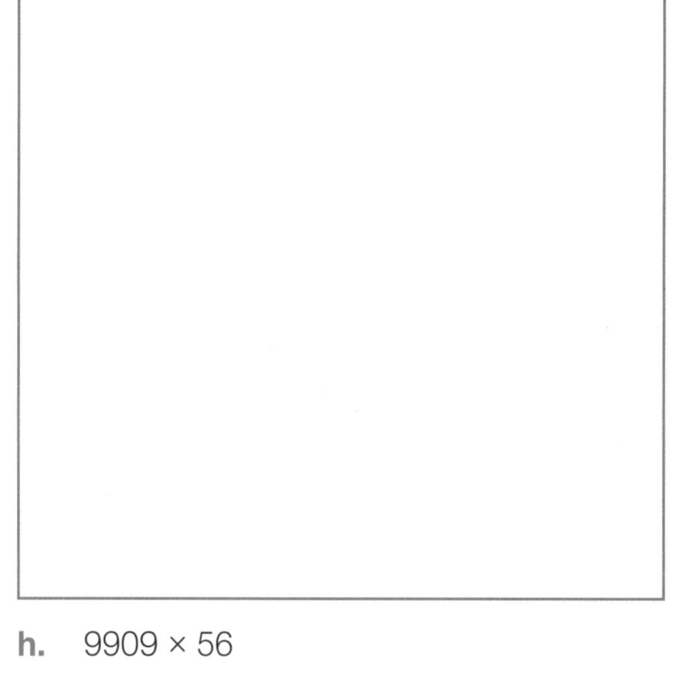

g. 3002 × 73

h. 9909 × 56

Long multiplication problem

It is important that you use the compact written method for long multiplication, as shown on page 24. Make sure you include all your working out.

How many slices of bread would you eat in 25 years? 10,000? 20,000? More? Less? Now is you chance to find out!

1. First of all, write an estimate here: _______________ slices of bread.
2. What calculation strategies could help you? What will you need to do first? Use the box below to write down some ideas.

3. Now use long multiplication to complete your calculations.

4. I eat _______________ slices of bread in 25 years.
5. Do you eat more or less than you estimated? _______________

Show time

The All-Star Production Company is working out how much money they will make from ticket sales in different sections of seating at their next live performance.

1. Set down each calculation in full and use long multiplication to work out your answers. Make sure the correct digits are lined up underneath each other.

a. £12 ticket sold to 127 people.

b. £25 ticket sold to 475 people.

c. £32 ticket sold to 1472 people.

d. £45 ticket sold to 2053 people.

e. £28 ticket sold to 4575 people.

School trip division

$$\begin{array}{r} 3\ 2 \\ 6\overline{)1\ 9^{1}2} \end{array}$$

When you do short division, make sure you keep the digits in the correct columns. In this example (192 divided by 6), 6 into 19 goes 3 times with one 10 left over. The 3 is written in the 10s column and the one 10 is carried over to the 1s, joining with the 2 to make 12; when 12 is divided by 6, it goes twice with no remainder.

Here are the ticket prices for the different school trips that have been arranged for the summer term.

1. If this was the money collected for each trip, work out how many tickets were bought by the pupils.

a. Theatre £376

Answer: ______________ tickets

b. Water World £675

Answer: ______________ tickets

c. Safari Park £1164

Answer: ____________ tickets

d. Concert £882

Answer: ____________ tickets

e. Football match £1170

Answer: ____________ tickets

f. Theme Park £1344

Answer: ____________ tickets

Round up and down

Some divisions will need to be rounded up or down, depending on the context.

230 people need to travel on 18-seater buses. How many buses are needed? This answer will be rounded up as you will need to seat all the people. 230 ÷ 18 = 12, remainder 14. So 13 buses are needed.

230 pens are packed 18 to each box. How many complete boxes are there? This answer will be rounded down as the question asks for the number of *complete* boxes: 12 boxes.

1. Calculate the answer to each question. There will be a remainder. Decide whether you need to round the answer up or down to answer the question.

a. A garden centre plants seedlings in trays of 35. How many complete trays can be filled with 456 seedlings?

_____ trays

b. Crayons are packed in boxes of 15. How many full boxes can be made from a pile of 456 crayons?

_____ boxes

c. Thirty-eight people can sit in a row of seats at the hockey stadium. How many rows are needed to seat 1200 spectators?

_____ rows

d. A jug holds 750ml of liquid. How many jugs will be needed to hold 8 litres of orange juice?

_____ jugs

e. A bus company has 28-seater buses. If 520 people want to go on a trip to the zoo, how many buses are needed to take them?

_____ buses

Divide the bill

These questions are set in a money context. You may need to consider remainders so that answers are given to the nearest pound. You will also have to decide whether to round remainders up or down to the nearest pound.

Marco's Restaurant specialises in catering for parties of people.

Here are the total bills for some of the parties.

1. Find out how much each person in each party will have to pay if the bills are shared out equally.

a. Bill £138, guests 6

b. Bill £208, guests 8

c. Bill £126, guests 9

2. For these questions, round the amounts up or down to the nearest pound.

a. Bill £189, guests 11

b. Bill £146, guests 7

c. Bill £393, guests 12

Long division

```
   2 4
18|4 4 7
  3 6 0   18 × 20
    8 7
    7 2   18 × 4
    1 5
```

$\frac{15}{18} = \frac{5}{6}$

Answer: $24\frac{5}{6}$

In long division it is very important to keep the columns correctly positioned with 1s under 1s, 10s under 10s and so on.
First, divide 44 by 18. It goes twice, write 2 above the 10s column.
It does not go exactly, so work out 18 × 20 (360) and subtract it from 447 to get 87.
Then divide 87 by 18. It goes four times, write 4 above the 1s column.
It does not go exactly, so work out 18 × 4 (72) and subtract it from 87 to get 15.
Write the remainder as a fraction of the divisor, that is, the number you are dividing by (18 in this case). Finally, write the fraction in its lowest term. $\frac{15}{18}$ can be expressed as $\frac{5}{6}$.

1. Use long division to solve the following. If there is a remainder, state this as a fraction.

a. 360 ÷ 15

Answer: ______________

b. 476 ÷ 14

Answer: ______________

c. 986 ÷ 17

Answer: ______________

d. 1625 ÷ 25

Answer: ____________

e. 760 ÷ 16

Answer: ____________

f. 930 ÷ 24

Answer: ____________

g. 852 ÷ 18

Answer: ____________

h. 1030 ÷ 15

Answer: ____________

Long division target practice

Use your division skills to hit the target.

149
102
205
138
32
22
109
112
176
622

1. Choose a number from each bag. Each number can only be used once.
2. Use long division to make a number from the target board.
3. Estimate first, as it will help you to choose the correct pair of numbers. The first one has been done for you.

Remember: The first two digits to be divided are the most important to help with estimating as they will give you the first digit of the target number.

9 12 7
11 4 15
8 10 6 18

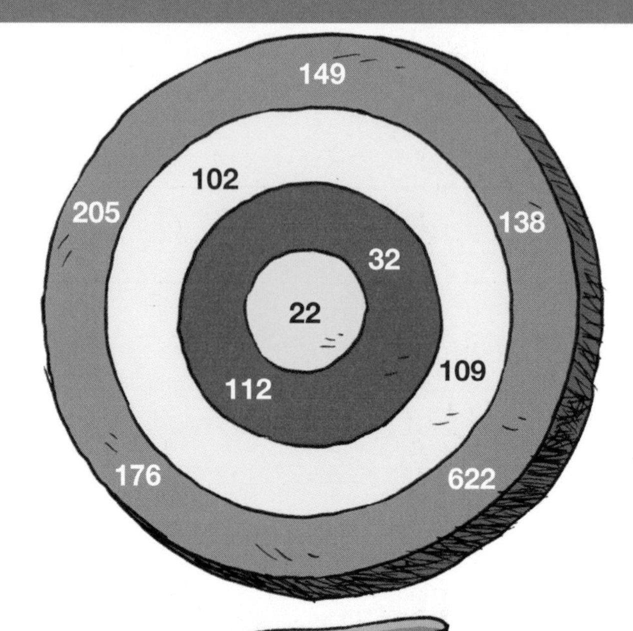

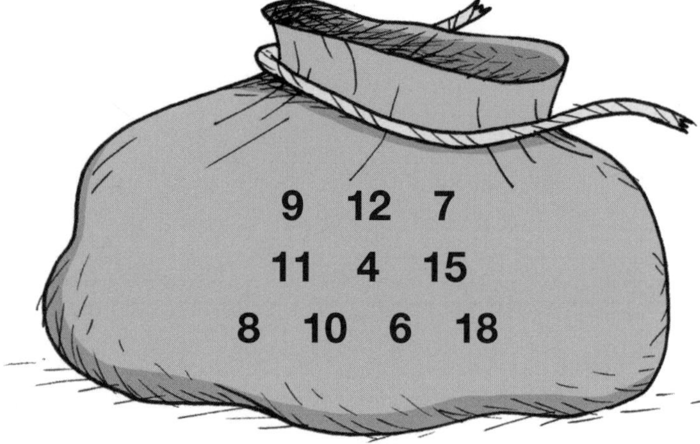

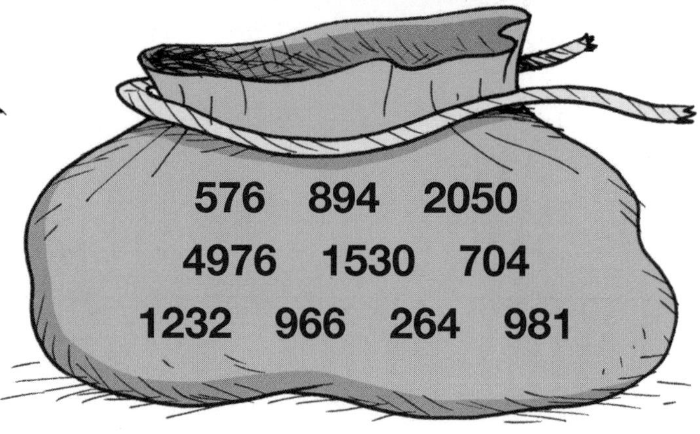

576 894 2050
4976 1530 704
1232 966 264 981

$\begin{array}{r}109\\9\overline{)981}\end{array}$				

Soup factory division

It is important to remember that both multiplication and subtraction are involved in the division process. It may help with a calculation if you work out some of the multiples of the divisor first by adding on. For example, multiples of 18 would be 18, 36, 54, 72, 90, and so on.

Rosa works in a soup factory, in the packaging section.

1. Use long division to calculate how many boxes she will need to pack the following flavours of soup. Show all your workings.

Remember: you may need to round up if there are tins left over.

a. **Tomato:** 1224 tins in boxes of 12

_______ boxes

b. **Chicken:** 1368 tins in boxes of 18

_______ boxes

c. **Oxtail:** 3227 tins in boxes of 15

_______ boxes

d. **Vegetable:** 3000 tins in boxes of 24

_______ boxes

e. **Minestrone:** 6989 tins in boxes of 32

_______ boxes

Adding order

Numbers can be added in any order and they will still produce the same total. Rearrange the order in your head before you start to add them mentally. It may be helpful to start with the largest number first and then continue going down in order of size.

1. Rearrange and then complete these calculations in your head so that you start with the largest amount. Remember to look for the number bonds.

a. 14 + 40 + 1210 + 56 + 17 = ______

b. 38 + 40 + 27 + 2750 + 33 = ______

c. 60 + 25 + 45 + 56 + 8530 = ______

d. 45 + 6480 + 70 + 42 + 58 = ______

e. 320km + 426km + 1580km = ______

f. 770kg + 4030kg + 659kg = ______

g. £942 + £840 + £9360 = ______

h. 220ml + 6780ml + 50ml = ______

2. Answer these questions. Think about putting the largest number first.

a. What amount results from adding £2.40, £4.60, £1.25 and £1.75?

______

b. Find the total of six, sixty, six hundred and six thousand and six.

______

c. Increase four hundred and seventy by five thousand, three hundred and thirty, and then increase the result by one million, three hundred and ten.

______

Bridging and adjusting

Round numbers, such as multiples of 10, 100 and 1000, can make lists of numbers easier to add. Numbers can always be rounded up to help with adding, and then the results adjusted to make the total correct:
572 + 389 = 572 + 400 – 11 = 972 – 11 = 961.

1. Write out the thinking stages when you answer these problems. Try to use the strategies outlined above.

a. 638 + 479 = ____________________

b. 914 + 587 = ____________________

c. 4523 – 2791 = ____________________

d. 3746 + 8973 = ____________________

2. Solve these problems using the same strategy as above.

a. Find the difference between £8259 and £2983. ____________________

b. Work out the total length in metres of 756cm and 988cm. ____________________

3. Fill in the thinking stages in these calculations.

a. 283 + 558 = 283 + 600 – __________ = __________ – 12 = 841

b. 837 – 589 = __________ – 600 + 11 = 237 + __________ = __________

c. 568 + __________ = 568 + 500 – 10 = __________ – __________ = 1058

Partition to add and multiply

Partitioning or splitting numbers into their component parts can help with both adding and multiplying. Remember that addition and multiplication are both commutative, which means the calculation can be done in any order.

This calculation shows the thinking stages for finding the correct answer:

356 + 475 = 300 + 400 + 50 + 70 + 6 + 5 = 700 + 120 + 11 = 831

1. Complete these two calculations and write out all the thinking stages in the same way as above.

a. 537 + 284 = ____________________

b. 168 + 642 = ____________________

2. Look at this calculation, then complete the following calculations in the same way.

478 + 453 = 478 + 22 + 431 = 500 + 431 = 931

a. 386 + 547 = ____________________

b. 584 + 343 = ____________________

c. 887 + 112 = ____________________

3. Look at the method of thinking in these examples, then complete the calculations below in the same way.

76 × 8 = (70 × 8) + (6 × 8) = 560 + 48 = 608

57 × 14 = (57 × 10) + (50 × 4) + (7 × 4) = 570 + 200 + 28 + 798

a. 59 × 7 = ____________________

b. 79 × 17 = ____________________

c. 96 × 19 = ____________________

d. 6 × 78 = ____________________

Using related multiplication and division facts

Doubling and halving can be helpful when carrying out some calculations.

- You can halve one number and then double the result:
  $20 \times 164 = 10 \times 164 \times 2 = 1640 \times 2 = 3280$.
- You can partition the number and double part of it and halve its result:
  $32 \times 15 = 32 \times 10 + 32 \times 10 \div 2 = 320 + 320 \div 2 = 320 + 160 = 480$.
- More difficult calcualtions can be made easier by doubling one number in the calculation and halving the result: $24 \times 15 = 24 \times 30 \div 2 = 720 \div 2 = 360$.

To multiply by 50, multiply by 100 and halve the result. To multiply by 25, multiply by 100 and divide the result by 4.

1. Complete these calculations using doubling and halving.

a. $23 \times 15 =$ ____________________

b. $35 \times 14 =$ ____________________

c. $45 \times 21 =$ ____________________

d. $125 \times 14 =$ ____________________

e. $120 \times 16 =$ ____________________

f. $121 \times 16 =$ ____________________

g. $225 \times 18 =$ ____________________

2. Now try to complete these calculations mentally.

a. $326 \times 50 =$ ____________________

b. $485 \times 50 =$ ____________________

c. $52 \times 25 =$ ____________________

d. $64 \times 25 =$ ____________________

Order of operations

Whenever calculations appear inside brackets, they must be done first. The order of operations is then as follows:

Brackets, Indices, Division, Multiplication, Addition and Subtraction.

We call this BIDMAS to help us remember. If there are several multiplications and divisions or additions and subtractions, do them one at a time from left to right.

1. Work out the answers to these problems.

a. (4 × 2) + 3 ____________

b. (2 × 3) – (8 – 5) ____________

c. 7 + (10 – 5) ____________

d. (13 – 9) × (4 + 2) ____________

2. Put brackets in these calculations to make them correct.

a. 2 + 4 × 3 = 14

b. 5 + 4 × 3 = 27

c. 10 – 3 × 3 = 21

d. 14 + 4 ÷ 2 = 9

e. 12 ÷ 3 + 1 = 3

f. 24 ÷ 2 + 4 = 4

3. Use the following numbers + – × and ÷) and brackets to make number statements that give the target answer.

a. 14, 6, 5, target 4 ____________

b. 12, 8, 3, target 12 ____________

c. 30, 6, 2, target 7 ____________

d. 3, 2, 4, target 2 ____________

4. Work out the answers using the correct order of operations.

a. 2 × 5 + 6 ____________

b. 5 × 3 – 6 × 2 ____________

c. 15 – 6 × 2 ____________

d. (6 + 4) × 5 – 3 ____________

Operations with brackets

Remember BIDMAS to make sure that you are carrying out operations in the correct order. When indices are used, remember that squaring a number means multiplying by itself, not multiplying by two.

1. Work out the answers to these calculations. Do any parts in brackets first.

a. (38m + 26m) – 52m = ______

b. 120km – (34km + 47km) = ______

c. £1350 + (£1240 – £325) = ______

d. How much must be added to £82.32 to make £90? ______

e. Find a quarter of a million, double the answer and add 150,000 to the result. Give the answer in words.

______

f. $(17 \times 2) - (6 \times 4) =$ ______

g. $7 + (48 \div 3) + 5 =$ ______

h. $2^2 \times 5 \times 6 =$ ______

i. $(6 + 3^2) \div 5 =$ ______

2. Use the following numbers with +, –, ×, ÷ and brackets to make number sentences that give the target answers.

a. 5, 5, 2, target 35 ______

b. 10, 8, 6, target 140 ______

c. 20, 3, 4, target 8 ______

d. 4, 4, 3, 2, target 26 ______

Mental calculations using mixed operations (1)

Remember to work out calculations inside brackets first and then follow the remaining order of operations. Work out the side of the equation that will produce an answer and use that information to find the missing amounts.

1. Complete these calculations. Do any parts in brackets first.

a. (28p ÷ 7) × 10 = 13p + ______________

b. 4cm × ______________ = 83cm – 51cm

c. ______________ = £91 – £14 – £12 + £27

d. (240g ÷ ______________) – (12g + 44g) = 24g

e. 60ml ÷ 5 = 120ml ÷ ______________

f. (59km + 21km) + (42km ÷ 6) = ______________

g. (83m – ______________) + (33m ÷ 3) = 76m

h. ______________ = (57p + 13p) ÷ (5 × 7)

i. 7cm × 5 = ______________ – 46cm

j. (84m + 25m) – (15m + 21m) = ______________

k. ______________ ÷ 4 = 88kg ÷ 11

l. 24g = (13g × 5) – 14g – ______________ – 15g

2. Read these problems and then write down the answers.

a. To the product of 1300 and 4, add 6850. ______________

b. Find $\frac{5}{8}$ of 640 and subtract one hundred and twenty-six from your answer. ______________

Mental calculations using mixed operations (2)

If there are no brackets in a problem, follow the remaining orders of operations as given in BIDMAS. If there are two sets of brackets, it does not matter which one you work out first, although it is usual to move from left to right.

1. Complete these calculations. Remember to do any parts in brackets first.

a. 81cm – 13cm = 34cm × ________

b. 21p + 14p + 23p – ________ = 47p

c. ________ = (9g × 8) – (2 × 7g)

d. (£63 ÷ 7) × (56 ÷ 4) = ________ + £26

e. 360g = (113g – 11g – 12g) × ________

f. (72km ÷ 8) × ________ = 150km – 51km

g. 900m = (90m ÷ ________ ÷ 5) × 450

h. ________ – 22p – 26p + 36p = 122p

i. (51cm + 28cm – ________ ÷ 2) = 29cm

j. £33 + £27 = £79 – ________

k. ________ + 14m + 16m – 23m = 118m

l. (6mm × 9) + (53mm – 29mm) = ________

2. Read these problems and work out the answers.

a. To the sum of 3600, 450 and 125, add three hundred and twenty-five.

____

b. From the sum of 2700, 520 and 80, subtract four hundred and eighty-eight.

____

c. Multiply five by ninety-eight and double the answer. ________________

d. Work out a third of six hundred and seventy-five shared by three. ________________

Mental calculations using mixed operations (3)

1. For each pair of numbers in the first column, multiply the two numbers together and write the result in the next column. Next add 225, divide by 5 and then subtract 21. Write down each result. The first one has been done for you.

		Multiply	+ 225	÷ 5	− 21
a.	45, 3	135	360	72	51
b.	5, 35				
c.	25, 12				
d.	7, 55				
e.	75, 5				
f.	3, 65				
g.	32, 5				
h.	10, 17				

2. Using the +, −, ×, ÷ and = signs make up six problems that all have at least four different signs in them, for example, (46 − 17) + (33 ÷ 3) + (7 × 8) = 96. The signs can be in any order. You will need to use brackets.

____

____

____

____

____

____

Mental calculations using mixed operations (4)

1. Work through these problems, following the sequence of operations in each one. The first one has been done for you.

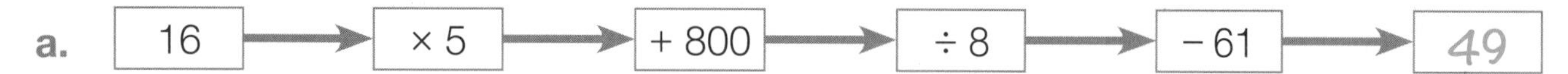

	Start	→	→	→	→	Result
a.	16	× 5	+ 800	÷ 8	− 61	49
b.	340	− 41	× 3	+ 3	÷ 5	
c.	4800	÷ 12	− 255	× 2	+ 709	
d.	2250	+ 4	÷ 7	− 121	× 5	
e.	25	× 9	+ 15	÷ 6	− 19	

2. Add together the two numbers in the first column and write the result in the next column. Next subtract 20, halve that answer and then multiply by 5. Write down each result. The first one has been done for you.

		Add	− 20	Halve	× 5
a.	43, 67	110	90	45	225
b.	56, 84				
c.	82, 78				
d.	69, 81				
e.	97, 93				
f.	36, 48				
g.	29, 35				
h.	59, 17				
i.	24, 68				
j.	35, 27				

Postal addition problem

Josh and Raj have some packages to post to different countries. They have a sheet of 5p stamps, a sheet of 16p stamps and a sheet of 23p stamps.

- Josh says: "I don't know how much the postage is for each of these packages but it is somewhere between 30p and 40p."
- Raj says: "That's OK, as there is only one amount over 30p that we can't make with these stamps."

1. Is Raj right? Show, with workings, which amounts between 30p and 40p you can make using 5p, 16p, and 23p stamps. It may help to try out some amounts on scrap paper first before starting to fill in the boxes on the page.

Amount	5p	16p	23p	Workings
30p				
31p				
32p				
33p				
34p				
35p				
36p				
37p				
38p				
39p				
40p				

Missing information problems

1. **There is an important piece of information missing from each of these word problems. Decide what information you need before the problems can be solved.**
2. **When you have decided what piece of information is missing, make up numbers for this part of the question and solve the problem. Show all your calculations. Estimate each answer first, and then find a way of checking it afterwards.**

a. Alan, Sunil, Martha and Emma collect football cards. If Alan has 57 cards, Sunil 29 cards and Martha 63 cards, how many cards do the four children have altogether?

b. Maths lessons take place each day in school. How long do maths lessons last in total during a normal school week?

c. A farmer divides 345 sheep into equal numbers to put them into pens. How many sheep are there in each pen?

d. Stacey is training for a swimming race. She swims 500 metres every weekday, but more at weekends. How far does she swim in a complete week?

Estimating costs

1. Estimate the cost of these tickets. You can round the prices to the nearest £10, £50 or £100.

a. Four tickets to Greece ______________

b. Three tickets to USA ______________

c. Five tickets to Spain ______________

d. Two tickets to France and three tickets to Spain ______________

2. Now work out the exact cost. How close were your estimates?

a.

b.

c.

d.

Addition and subtraction problem

You can use a variety of mental and written methods for addition and subtraction to work out the answers to problems. Always make sure digits are kept in the correct columns.

Professor Find-It and his assistant Doctor Dig-It-Up have been working deep in the jungle. Unfortunately, they have both come down with a bad case of swamp fever. They have managed to get back to the first aid centre, but need a little help getting to the medicine chest.

- In order to get to the medicine, they need to cross the river using the stepping stones.
- The stones they choose must add up to exactly 1000.
- Help them choose the correct stones to cross the river. (They don't have to use adjoining stones; they are allowed to jump to stones a little further away.) Remember to keep a note of the numbers you have used.

1. Colour in the stones that add up to exactly 1000. Remember, you can jump over stones.

2. Now that they have crossed the river, they need help to open the medicine chest. They need to find out a secret code to open the chest. Work out the secret code by calculating the answers to these questions. Write each answer in the space provided. Good luck – the explorers are counting on you.

6483 − 1372	9023 − 4362	7001 − 4921	5091 − 3275
______	______	______	______
______	______	______	______

Wedding madness!

To solve a multi-step problem, work out questions one step at a time. Read each step carefully and decide on the calculation needed. Jot down information you need to remember and always check your answers.

1. Footballer Gary Goalie is marrying Mystique from the pop group Flirty Foxes. Work out the total cost of their wedding. Use the box below to make jottings.

There will be 480 guests at the wedding.

- A seven-course meal: £52 per head
- 1200 bottles of champagne: £30 each
- The band will play for 3 hours: £3250 per hour
- 120 flower arrangements: £28 each
- 212 taxis: £15 each

Total cost = ______

2. However, Gary plays for lowly Dumpton Town and gets paid £300 per week. How many weeks will it take Gary to pay for the wedding?

______ weeks

Jottings:

Use your squares

Squaring a number is multiplying it by itself, for example 12 squared or $12^2 = 12 \times 12 = 144$. When squaring multiples of 10, make sure that the number of zeros in the answer matches the number of zeros in the question, for example 60×60 has two zeros, so there must be two zeros in the answer: $60 \times 60 = 3600$.

Use your knowledge of square numbers to help you solve these problems.

1. Rashid says: "$12 \times 12 = 144$, so 12×13 must equal 157."

a. Is he correct? ______________________________

b. Explain your reasoning. ______________________________

2. Mr Smith's garden measures 49m by 52m.

a. What is the garden's approximate area? ______________________________

b. Explain how you worked this out. ______________________________

3. Molly says: "To find the answer to 70^2, you multiply 7×7, then add the zero. The answer is 490."

a. Is she correct? ______________________________

b. Explain your answer. ______________________________

4. What number multiplied by itself gives the answer 6400? ______________________________

5. Sunnyville School's playground measures 40m by 40m. A space measuring 18m by 22m is marked out for ball games. Approximately how much space is left for other types of games? Show your workings.

____

____

____

Home decorating

When doing calculations using amounts with decimal points in them, make sure the decimal points are lined up underneath each other.

Look at the question carefully and don't forget that you may need to round the answer up or down.

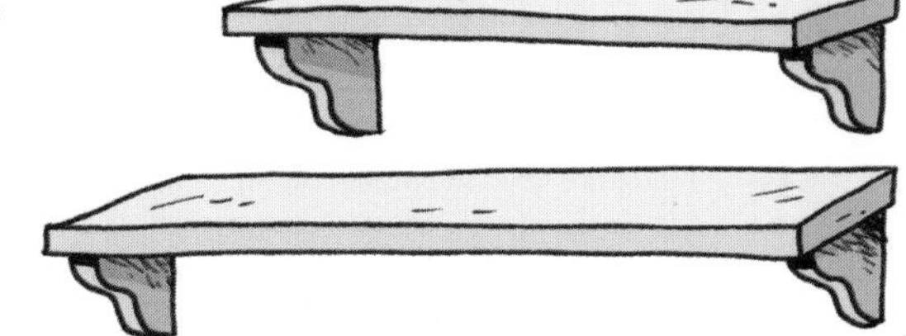

1. Fiona wants three new shelves for her bathroom.
   The shelves need to be 1.75m long, 2.8m long and 1.35m long.
   A length of wood measuring 3.5m long costs £8.99.
   Each shelf needs two brackets.
   Brackets cost £3.89 each.
   How much will it cost Fiona to put up her shelves?

Total £ ______

2. A tin holds 1.5 litres of paint.
   One tin is enough to cover an area of 9 square metres.
   The total surface area of the living room wall is 59 square metres.

   How many tins does Fiona need to paint the living room? ______

   How many litres of paint will this be? ______

Total ______ litres

Measure up

Help the staff of Meadow Lane Primary School with their work. Read through the questions carefully, picking out the key words and numbers for your calculations. Work out approximate answers first. You may need to make jottings as you are working through the calculations. Check your answers at the end.

1. Mrs Jones has to cover a large display board in the hall with frieze paper. The paper comes in rolls 50cm wide and 4m long. The display board is 10m long and 2m high. How many rolls of paper will she need? ______

2. Mr Price needs to paint the kick wall in the playground bright green. One litre of paint covers an area of 3 square metres. The kick wall measures 8m by $1\frac{1}{2}$m. How many litres of paint will he need? ______

3. The school day starts at 8.50am and ends at 3.15pm. There is a playtime break at 10.40am until 10.55am and a lunch break from 12 noon until 1.05pm.
   - **a.** How long is the school day? ______
   - **b.** How long do the children spend in lessons each day? ______
   - **c.** How much playtime do the children have in a week? ______

4. The school has a Healthy Eating Tuck Shop. This is what they sell:

Fruit pot 20p	Wholemeal toast 15p
Fruit juice 10p	Pot of raisins 15p

   - **a.** On the first day of school, 75 children buy a fruit pot and 59 children buy toast. How much money does Mrs Lemon, the cook, make? ______
   - **b.** On the second day, £8.50 is spent on fruit juice and £9.30 on raisins. How many of each were sold? ______

You choose the problem

Remember that in any number sentence, calculations inside brackets must be done first. When using the four operations +, −, ×, ÷ with decimal numbers think carefully about where the decimal point will go in the answer.

1. Make up a word problem for each of these calculations. Try to use a good variety of words. Write the answer.

a. $(21 + 7) \times 8$

b. $20.5 \div 5 - 0.75$

c. £6.99 × 4 + £2.35

Estimate before solving

When solving word problems, decide which methods you need to use. Can you solve the problems using mental methods with jottings, or do you need formal written methods? Estimate an answer first and remember to check your solution at the end.

Find the correct operations to solve these word problems involving numbers and quantities. Remember to find approximate answers first and check your results at the end.

1. There are 456 children in the school. 213 have a packed lunch, 54 go home and the rest have school dinners. How many children have school dinners?

2. Alan cycles 8.3km twice a day as he travels to and from school. How far does he travel in a 15-week school term?

3. A dog weighs 8.27kg. How many grams must it gain to weigh 14kg?

4. It costs Sarah's mum £46 to fill her car tank with petrol. She travels an average of 250 miles on each tank. How many full tanks of petrol will she need to cover 2750 miles? How much will this cost her?

What's wrong?

If you estimate an answer first you will have an idea of what the solution should be.
One way of checking the answer and spotting errors would be to use the inverse operation, for example, if we know that 75 + 96 = 171, then it follows that 171 – 96 = 75.

1. Each of these answers has mistakes in them. Estimate each answer, check it through carefully and correct any errors.

a. $\begin{array}{r} 253 \\ +\underline{647} \\ \underline{902} \end{array}$	**b.** $\begin{array}{r} 3476 \\ +\underline{1885} \\ \underline{5461} \end{array}$
c. $\begin{array}{r} 471.3 \\ +\underline{526.4} \\ \underline{887.7} \end{array}$	**d.** $\begin{array}{r} 732 \\ -\underline{329} \\ \underline{413} \end{array}$
e. $\begin{array}{r} 89.52 \\ -\underline{16.68} \\ \underline{61.84} \end{array}$	**f.** $\begin{array}{r} £50.00 \\ -\underline{£29.99} \\ \underline{£20.11} \end{array}$

Ink blots

Estimating answers first will give you some idea of what they should be. To find the missing numbers, use the fact that multiplication is the inverse of division and vice versa, for example, if we know that 235 × 7 = 1645 then it follows that 1645 ÷ 235 = 7 and 1645 ÷ 7 = 235.

1. Davinder has been very messy with his work today. His pen is leaking and ink blots have dropped on some of the digits. Find the digit that has been covered with ink in each calculation and write it in the box. Use known facts and estimation to help you.

a.

```
   147
×    4
  58*
```

b.

```
  2*96
×    5
 12980
```

c.

```
£ 15.30
×     *
£107.10
```

d.

```
   856
3 | 25*8
```

e.

```
   *51
8 | 2008
```

f.

```
   7.30
9 | £6*.70
```

Day trip

With multi-step problems it will help to keep jottings of all your working out.

5% of an amount can be calculated by working out 10% and then halving it. For $12\frac{1}{2}$% find 10% first and then halve 5% to find the extra $2\frac{1}{2}$%. For example $12\frac{1}{2}$% of 600 is 60 + 15 = 75.

The youth club plan a day trip to a theme park.

- The cost of the coach is £650. There are 54 seats.
- They calculate that if they sell 50 tickets at £13 each they will break even.
- They decide that if the coach is full, they will be able to give everyone a discount.
- The coach is full, so when they count the fares they decide to give everyone a refund of 5% and to give the balance to the driver as a tip.

1. How much does each passenger get back?

____

2. How much does the driver get?

____

3. At the theme park it costs £12 entry per person, but there is a group discount of $12\frac{1}{2}$%.

a. How much will each person pay?

____

b. What is the total cost for the day for each person?

____

Ferry crossing

Study this table of ferry prices before attempting the questions.

Month	Car plus two passengers	Motorcycle plus rider	Adult foot passenger	Child foot passenger
January	99	49	22	11
February	99	49	22	11
March	99	49	22	11
April	130	65	25	15
May	130	65	25	15
June	130	65	25	15
July	150	70	30	18
August	150	70	30	18
September	130	65	25	15
October	100	49	22	11
November	100	49	22	11
December	100	49	22	11
Prices for a single crossing				
Additional adults in a car £5 All children under 15yrs in a car travel free				
Mini-break – up to five days abroad 40% discount				
Saver – up to ten days abroad 20% discount				

1. How much does it cost for a family of two adults and three children aged under 15, travelling by car, for a two-week trip, leaving in August and returning in September?

2. Calculate the cost for a mini-break of four days in May for four adults in a car.

3. How much does it cost for two adults to take their car for eight days in October?

4. What will the fare be for two adults and three children without a car, travelling for two weeks in June?

Common factors and simplifying fractions

A common factor is a factor that is common to two or more numbers.
To simplify a fraction, or reduce it to its lowest terms, you need to divide the numerator and denominator by a common factor.

For $\frac{12}{15}$: 3 is a common factor of both 12 and 15, as 3 into 12 will go 4 times and 3 into 15 will go 5 times. So $\frac{12}{15}$ can be simplified to $\frac{4}{5}$.

The highest common factor (HCF) is the largest factor that is common to a set of any given numbers. For 16 and 24, the common factors are 2, 4 and 8, so the HCF is 8.

1. Write all the common factors of each pair of numbers.

a. 6, 10: ______

b. 12, 20: ______

c. 8, 10: ______

d. 12, 36: ______

e. 8, 12: ______

f. 45, 30: ______

g. 16, 18: ______

h. 50, 40: ______

2. Write down the highest common factor of each pair of numbers.

a. 9, 12: ______

b. 20, 50: ______

c. 15, 20: ______

d. 28, 42: ______

e. 20, 16: ______

f. 32, 48: ______

g. 30, 24: ______

h. 60, 40: ______

3. Simplify the following fractions to their lowest terms. This will mean dividing the numerator and denominator by the HCF.

a. $\frac{6}{8}$ = ______________________ b. $\frac{5}{10}$ = ______________________

c. $\frac{4}{12}$ = ______________________ d. $\frac{15}{25}$ = ______________________

e. $\frac{20}{30}$ = ______________________ f. $\frac{60}{100}$ = ______________________

g. $\frac{9}{27}$ = ______________________ h. $\frac{20}{24}$ = ______________________

i. $\frac{14}{42}$ = ______________________ j. $\frac{36}{40}$ = ______________________

k. $\frac{16}{36}$ = ______________________ l. $\frac{95}{100}$ = ______________________

4. Simplify the following improper fractions. Change them to whole or mixed numbers first.

a. $\frac{18}{3}$ = ______________________ b. $\frac{10}{9}$ = ______________________

c. $\frac{12}{10}$ = ______________________ d. $\frac{21}{5}$ = ______________________

e. $\frac{38}{4}$ = ______________________ f. $\frac{26}{10}$ = ______________________

g. $\frac{39}{9}$ = ______________________ h. $\frac{51}{12}$ = ______________________

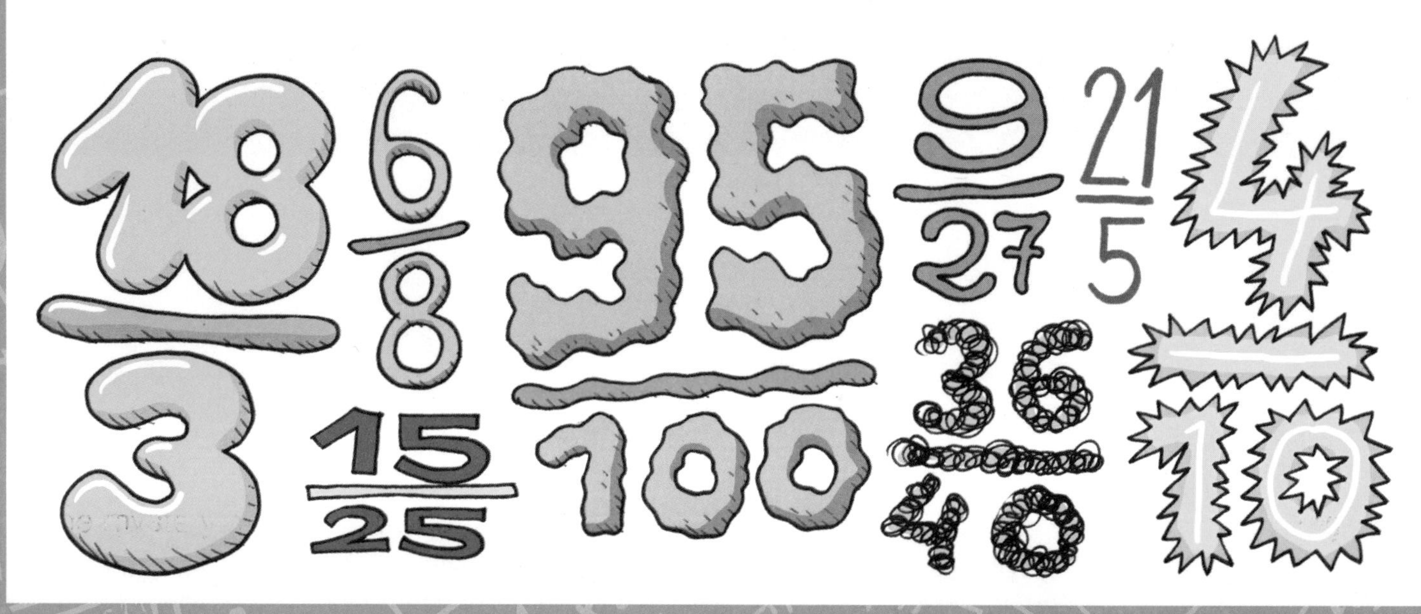

Comparing fractions

Which is larger, $\frac{5}{6}$ or $\frac{3}{4}$? This would be easy to answer if they had the same denominator. A common multiple of both denominators is 12.

To turn 6 into 12 you multiply it by 2, so do the same to the top number: $\frac{5}{6}$ becomes $\frac{10}{12}$.
To turn 4 into 12 you multiply it by 3, so do the same to the top number: $\frac{3}{4}$ becomes $\frac{9}{12}$.
$\frac{10}{12} > \frac{9}{12}$ so $\frac{5}{6}$ is larger than $\frac{3}{4}$.

1. Compare each pair of fractions by converting them to fractions with a common denominator. Then write the correct sign, < or >, between each pair.

a. $\frac{1}{2}$ and $\frac{5}{8}$ ______

b. $\frac{3}{5}$ and $\frac{2}{3}$ ______

c. $\frac{2}{3}$ and $\frac{3}{4}$ ______

d. $\frac{4}{5}$ and $\frac{3}{4}$ ______

e. $\frac{5}{6}$ and $\frac{7}{9}$ ______

f. $\frac{4}{5}$ and $\frac{5}{9}$ ______

g. $\frac{7}{10}$ and $\frac{9}{20}$ ______

h. $\frac{7}{8}$ and $\frac{11}{12}$ ______

2. Put these groups of fractions in order of size, smallest to largest. Use the same method as above.

a. $\frac{2}{3}$, $\frac{1}{6}$, $\frac{3}{4}$ ______

b. $\frac{5}{9}$, $\frac{2}{3}$, $\frac{11}{18}$ ______

c. $\frac{1}{2}$, $\frac{7}{12}$, $\frac{5}{6}$ ______

d. $\frac{1}{4}$, $\frac{5}{12}$, $\frac{2}{3}$ ______

Equal match

Equivalent fractions have equal value but different numerators and denominators.

Find equivalent fractions by multiplying or dividing the numerator and the denominator by the same number, For example; $\frac{5}{7}$ is equivalent to $\frac{10}{14}$ (double both numbers); $\frac{12}{15}$ is equivalent to $\frac{4}{5}$ (divide both numbers by 3).

1. Match the equivalent values. One has been done for you.

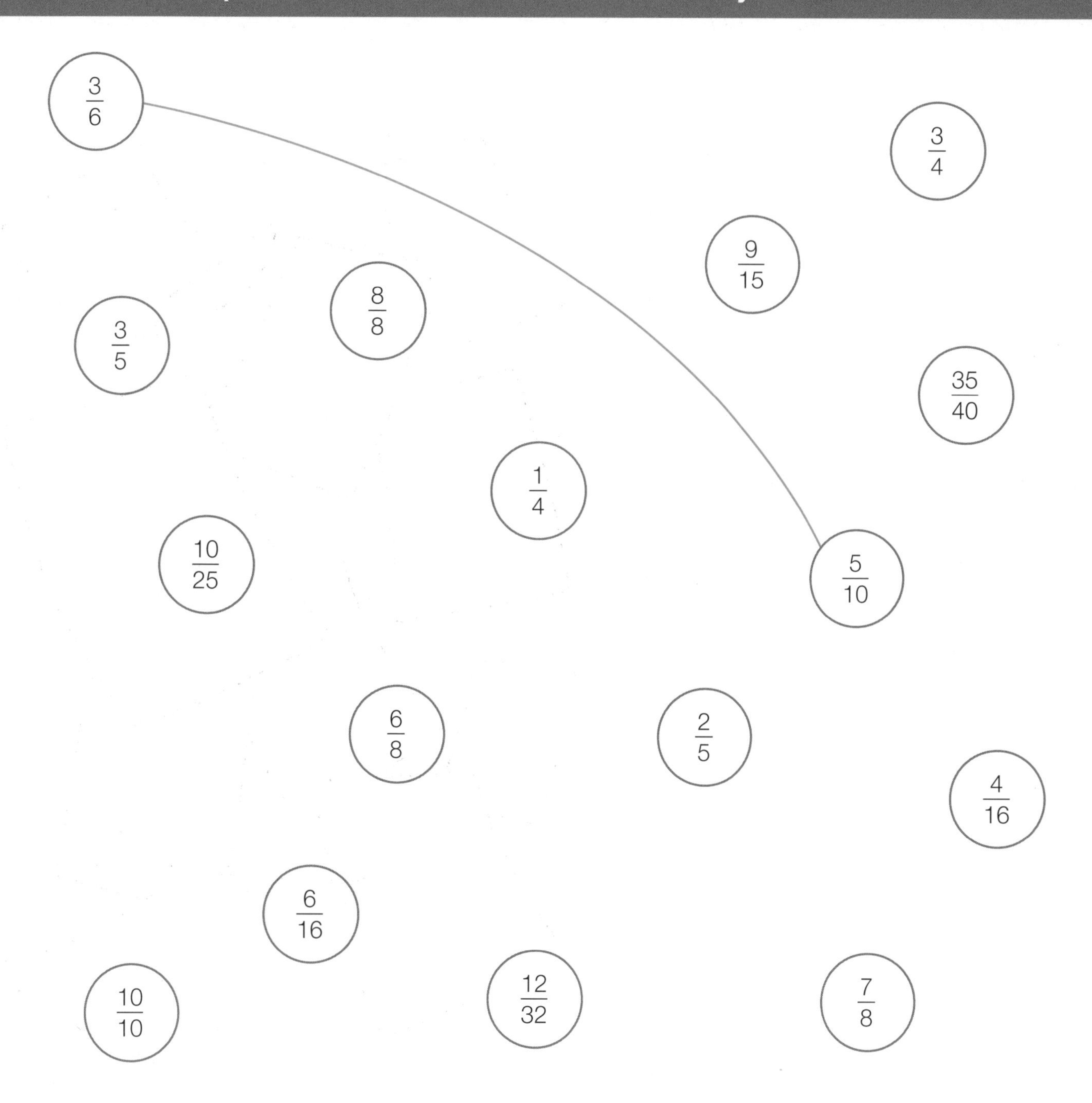

Add and subtract fractions

It is easy to add or subtract fractions if they have the same denominator,
For example, $\frac{3}{5} + \frac{1}{5} = \frac{4}{5}$ and $\frac{5}{6} - \frac{4}{6} = \frac{1}{6}$.
If they have different denominators then first convert them so they have a common denominator, for example, $\frac{2}{5} + \frac{3}{10} = \frac{4}{10} + \frac{3}{10} = \frac{7}{10}$ and $\frac{5}{6} - \frac{1}{4} = \frac{10}{12} - \frac{3}{12} = \frac{7}{12}$.

1. Work out each fraction problem by finding a common denominator.

a. $\frac{4}{5} + \frac{7}{10} =$ ______ + ______ = ______

b. $\frac{1}{2} - \frac{3}{8} =$ ______ − ______ = ______

c. $\frac{1}{2} - \frac{3}{10} =$ ______ − ______ = ______

d. $\frac{4}{5} + \frac{1}{2} =$ ______ + ______ = ______

e. $\frac{7}{12} + \frac{3}{4} =$ ______ + ______ = ______

f. $\frac{5}{8} - \frac{1}{4} =$ ______ − ______ = ______

g. $\frac{7}{10} - \frac{3}{5} =$ ______ − ______ = ______

h. $\frac{2}{3} + \frac{3}{4} =$ ______ + ______ = ______

i. $\frac{1}{2} + \frac{3}{5} =$ ______ + ______ = ______

j. $\frac{5}{8} + \frac{7}{12} =$ ______ + ______ = ______

k. $\frac{1}{2} - \frac{1}{3} =$ ______ − ______ = ______

l. $\frac{7}{8} - \frac{3}{4} =$ ______ − ______ = ______

m. $\frac{11}{12} - \frac{1}{4} =$ ______ − ______ = ______

Adding and subtracting mixed numbers

When adding and subtracting mixed numbers, the whole numbers must be dealt with first. Then change the fraction parts to fractions with the same denominator before adding or subtracting. For example:

$2\frac{1}{2} + 1\frac{7}{8} = 3 + \frac{4}{8} + \frac{7}{8} = 3\frac{11}{8} = 4\frac{3}{8}$ Or $3\frac{2}{3} - 1\frac{1}{2} = 2\frac{4}{6} - \frac{3}{6} = 2\frac{1}{6}$

1. Work out these additions and subtractions by first adding or subtracting the whole numbers and then finding the common denominator to add or subtract the fractional part.

a. $2\frac{1}{8} + 3\frac{2}{8} =$ ________________

b. $6\frac{1}{5} - 1\frac{1}{5} =$ ________________

c. $3\frac{1}{8} + 1\frac{3}{4} =$ ________________

d. $2\frac{1}{2} - \frac{1}{4} =$ ________________

e. $1\frac{3}{10} + 2\frac{3}{4} =$ ________________

f. $3\frac{7}{8} - 2\frac{1}{2} =$ ________________

g. $5\frac{2}{3} + 2\frac{7}{8} =$ ________________

h. $3\frac{3}{8} - 1\frac{1}{4} =$ ________________

i. $2\frac{3}{10} + 2\frac{7}{20} =$ ________________

j. $5\frac{7}{10} - 3\frac{1}{4} =$ ________________

k. $4\frac{7}{9} + 3\frac{5}{6} =$ ________________

l. $7\frac{4}{5} - 5\frac{2}{3} =$ ________________

Multiply pairs of fractions

When multiplying fractions, if no whole numbers are involved, you first multiply the numerators and then multiply the denominators. Look for ways to cancel down so that the answer is always written in its simplest form such as: $\frac{2}{5} \times \frac{3}{8} = \frac{6}{40} = \frac{3}{20}$.

Before multiplying whole or mixed numbers, change them into improper fractions.

So $5 \times \frac{3}{4} = \frac{5}{1} \times \frac{3}{4} = \frac{15}{4} = 3\frac{3}{4}$

$4\frac{2}{3} \times 1\frac{2}{7} = \frac{14}{3} \times \frac{9}{7} = \frac{126}{21} = 6$.

1. Multiply the following pairs of fractions.

a. $\frac{2}{5} \times \frac{1}{2} =$ ____________________

b. $\frac{3}{4} \times \frac{1}{12} =$ ____________________

c. $\frac{3}{4} \times \frac{2}{9} =$ ____________________

d. $\frac{5}{16} \times \frac{4}{5} =$ ____________________

e. $\frac{4}{9} \times \frac{3}{8} =$ ____________________

f. $\frac{5}{12} \times \frac{4}{5} =$ ____________________

g. $\frac{1}{3} \times \frac{9}{10} =$ ____________________

h. $\frac{2}{5} \times \frac{3}{4} =$ ____________________

i. $1\frac{1}{4} \times \frac{2}{5} =$ ______________________

j. $\frac{3}{5} \times 2\frac{1}{2} =$ ______________________

k. $\frac{4}{7} \times 1\frac{3}{4} =$ ______________________

l. $2\frac{3}{4} \times \frac{7}{11} =$ ______________________

m. $1\frac{7}{8} \times 1\frac{3}{5} =$ ______________________

n. $2\frac{2}{3} \times 1\frac{1}{2} =$ ______________________

o. $1\frac{7}{8} \times 2\frac{2}{5} =$ ______________________

p. $2\frac{2}{3} \times 2\frac{1}{4} =$ ______________________

q. $1\frac{3}{4} \times 1\frac{3}{7} =$ ______________________

r. $2\frac{1}{4} \times 1\frac{1}{6} =$ ______________________

s. $1\frac{4}{5} \times 1\frac{1}{4} =$ ______________________

t. $3\frac{1}{2} \times 1\frac{1}{5} =$ ______________________

Dividing proper fractions by a whole number

In a fraction, the inverse is made by the numerator changing position with the denominator. The inverse of 2 ($\frac{2}{1}$) is $\frac{1}{2}$ and the inverse of 8 ($\frac{8}{1}$) is $\frac{1}{8}$. Dividing by a number is the same as multiplying by its inverse; so $\frac{2}{3} \div 2$ is the same as $\frac{2}{3} \times \frac{1}{2} = \frac{2}{6}$ or $\frac{1}{3}$.

1. Divide these fractions by whole numbers.

a. $\frac{2}{3} \div 4 =$ __________

b. $\frac{2}{7} \div 2 =$ __________

c. $\frac{5}{6} \div 10 =$ __________

d. $\frac{4}{5} \div 8 =$ __________

e. $\frac{2}{7} \div 8 =$ __________

f. $\frac{5}{8} \div 10 =$ __________

g. $\frac{5}{9} \div 9 =$ __________

h. $\frac{12}{16} \div 6 =$ __________

i. $\frac{7}{8} \div 14 =$ __________

j. $\frac{5}{6} \div 15 =$ __________

k. $\frac{4}{7} \div 8 =$ __________

l. $\frac{11}{12} \div 4 =$ __________

Compare and order fractions > 1

To change an improper fraction into a mixed number, divide the denominator into the numerator. However many times it goes becomes the whole number, but the remainder stays as a fraction, for example $\frac{17}{5} = 3\frac{2}{5}$.
To change a mixed number into an improper fraction, multiply the whole number by the denominator, then add on the numerator, for example $4\frac{3}{8} = 4 \times 8 + 3 = \frac{35}{8}$.

Draw a line to match each mixed number with an equivalent improper fraction. Beware! Two cards do not have a partner.

1. Can you explain why the two remaining fractions do not match?

___

2. When you have matched all the pairs, write them in order, starting with the smallest.

___

$\frac{10}{7}$	$\frac{32}{9}$	$\frac{38}{16}$	$\frac{37}{5}$	$\frac{49}{12}$
$\frac{47}{9}$	$\frac{63}{12}$	$\frac{29}{5}$	$\frac{15}{7}$	$\frac{36}{16}$
$5\frac{3}{12}$	$5\frac{4}{5}$	$2\frac{1}{7}$	$4\frac{1}{12}$	$7\frac{2}{5}$
$2\frac{6}{16}$	$3\frac{5}{9}$	$1\frac{3}{7}$	$3\frac{4}{16}$	$5\frac{2}{9}$

Fraction action

To find a fraction of a number or an amount, you need to divide the number or amount by the denominator (to find the unit fraction) and then multiply the result by the numerator.
To find $\frac{2}{3}$ of 15: 15 ÷ 3 = 5 and 5 × 2 = 10. So $\frac{2}{3}$ of 15 is 10.

1. Complete these tables.

$\frac{5}{6}$	of	240m	
		15kg	
		£63	

$\frac{2}{3}$	of	1m 23cm	
		£156	
		174kg	

2. What is 25% of each of these amounts?

a. £200 ____________________

b. 3m ____________________

c. 10kg ____________________

3. What is 10% of each of these amounts?

a. £365 ____________________

b. 3m 50cm ____________________

c. $6\frac{1}{2}$ kg ____________________

Fractions of curtains

A remainder in a division calculation can always be shown as a fraction.

$25 \div 3 = 8$ r1 or $8\frac{1}{3}$.

To convert a remainder into a decimal number, put .00 after the number being divided and use short division to work out the answer to one decimal place.

$$3 \overline{)\,25.^{1}0^{1}0} = 8.33$$

or 8.3 to one decimal place.

Mrs Jones has bought a 24m roll of material and she wants to make curtains. She needs seven curtains, so she wants to divide the roll of material exactly by seven.

1. How much material will Mrs Jones have for each curtain? Give your answer as:

a. a fraction ______________________________

b. a decimal ______________________________

2. Give the answer to each of these division calculations as a fraction and as a decimal rounded to one decimal place.

a. $58 \div 7 =$ ______________________________

b. $71 \div 4 =$ ______________________________

c. $43 \div 8 =$ ______________________________

Equivalence bingo

Four people are playing a game of family bingo: Mr Lucky, Miss Chance, Ms Gamble and Mrs Bonus. Below is the set of clues that are going to be called out.

Clues

1. $\frac{1}{2}$ as a decimal
2. $\frac{1}{4}$ as a percentage
3. 10% as a fraction
4. 75% as a fraction
5. $\frac{8}{10}$ as a decimal
6. $\frac{6}{10}$ as a percentage
7. $\frac{3}{10}$ as a percentage
8. 0.5 as a fraction
9. 20% as a decimal
10. $\frac{1}{10}$ as a percentage
11. $\frac{3}{4}$ as a percentage
12. $\frac{7}{10}$ as a percentage

Work through the clues in the correct order, crossing off the answers on each of the cards to find out who is the winner of the game (that is, the player with all the numbers crossed off first).

Mr Lucky

90%	$\frac{3}{4}$	$\frac{1}{4}$	
		20%	$\frac{1}{10}$
75%	0.5		
			$\frac{1}{2}$

Miss Chance

0.2		40%	
	$\frac{1}{8}$		60%
		$\frac{1}{10}$	
0.5		0.7	$\frac{3}{4}$

Ms Gamble

25%			$\frac{3}{4}$
40%		10%	
	0.8		$\frac{1}{2}$
$\frac{1}{10}$			30%

Mrs Bonus

	0.5		$\frac{1}{10}$
$\frac{1}{2}$			0.8
	$\frac{3}{4}$	25%	
70%			30%

Who was the winner of the game? ______________________

Fraction match

It is important to remember that when you multiply by a fraction, the answer will be smaller, for example $\frac{2}{3}$ of £15 is £10.

Look carefully at the fraction calculation in the first column and match it with its answer in the second column. There are a number of answers here that are similar so make sure you work out calculations carefully. Check the position of decimal points.

A	$\frac{3}{4}$ of 2m 60cm
B	$\frac{2}{5}$ of 4m 90cm
C	$3\frac{1}{3}$ × £3.00
D	$\frac{1}{5}$ of £51
E	$2\frac{3}{4}$ × £3.60
F	$1\frac{1}{4}$ × $1\frac{1}{2}$m
G	$\frac{1}{3}$ of £30.90
H	$\frac{3}{8}$ of 5.1m
I	$\frac{2}{5}$ × £24
J	$2\frac{1}{2}$ × 77cm

1	192.5cm
2	191.25cm
3	£9.90
4	196cm
5	£9.60
6	£10.20
7	195cm
8	£10.30
9	£10
10	187.5cm

Percentage maker

Remember that 25% = $\frac{1}{4}$, 75% = $\frac{3}{4}$ and 60% = $\frac{6}{10}$. Remember that 15% can be found by finding 10% then halving it to give 5% and adding the two results together. Also, 60% will be six times greater than 10%.

Feed the numbers through the percentage machines to complete each chart. The first one has been partly filled in.

Credit crunch

Remember, 40% is 10% × 4 while 45% will be 10% × 4 + $\frac{1}{2}$ of 10%.
To find $\frac{3}{5}$ of an amount, divide the amount, by 5 and then multiply the result by 3.

Mrs Brown needs a new cooker. She has been looking at the different offers and is confused. Help her to find the best deal.

1. Budget Stores has a cooker on offer for £575, but will give a 40% discount for cash.

   How much will it cost? ____________________

2. Superstore has the same cooker on sale for £625, but will give a 45% discount.

   How much will it cost? ____________________

   Where should she buy her new cooker? ____________________

Mrs Brown also sees the new fridge that she wants in Budget Stores. This is priced at £280 but her husband says it is only $\frac{3}{5}$ of that price in Electro Discounts.

3. Should she buy it at Budget Stores with their 40% discount or should she buy at Electro

   Discounts? ____________________

Place value in decimals

1. Give the place value of the circled digits in each of the following numbers. Look carefully at the position of the decimal point.

a. 15.27 (circled: 5) ☐ b. 9.36 (circled: 3) ☐ c. 14.752 (circled: 5) ☐ d. 24.03 (circled: 3) ☐

e. 6.429 (circled: 9) ☐ f. 30.054 (circled: 3) ☐ g. 47.002 (circled: 7) ☐ h. 56.751 (circled: 7) ☐

2. What are the values of the letters X, Y and Z?

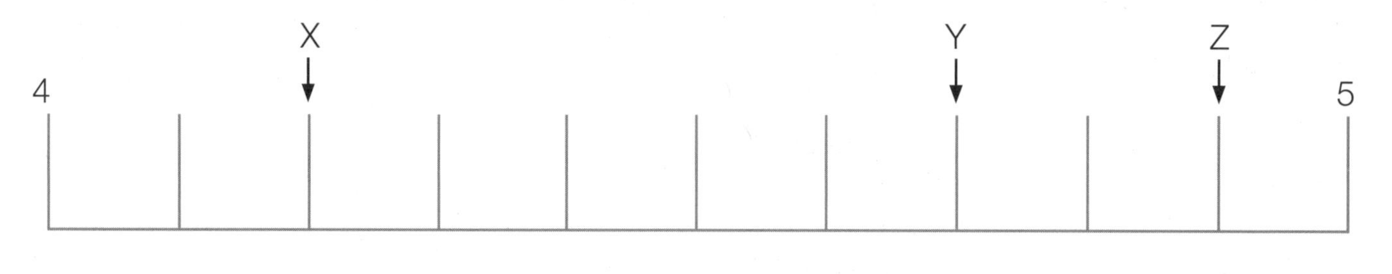

X ________ Y ________ Z ________

3. Draw arrows to show these numbers on the number line.

a. 15.05 b. 15.28 c. 15.35 d. 15.49

15 — 15.5

4. Draw arrows to show the approximate positions where these decimal numbers go on the scale. Be as accurate as you can.

a. 0.23 b. 1.72 c. 0.54 d. 1.09 e. 1.98

0 — 1 — 2

Ordering decimals

Remember to start reading the size of the decimal number from the left and work towards the right each time. If you are comparing numbers and the whole numbers are the same, look at the tenths. If the whole numbers and the tenths are the same, then look at the hundredths, and so on. So the following numbers in order, smallest first, would be 4.088, 5.088, 5.181, 5.186.

1. These are the scores achieved by five children playing the console game Guitar Genius. Write each child's scores in order, smallest first.

a. Eric: 2.553, 5.552, 5.225, 2.225

____

b. Josh: 1.002, 2.101, 1.221, 0.202

____

c. Ganesh: 5.445, 4.554, 4.504, 5.545

____

d. Katy: 13.367, 13.673, 31.352, 13.763

____

e. Alesha: 32.332, 23.223, 33.323, 23.322

____

Baking time

To scale ingredients up or down in correct proportions, find out how much is needed for one person and then multiply up or down. So 150g of butter for two people would be 75g of butter for one person, and 75g × 3 = 225g of butter for three people.

1. These are the ingredients needed for making currant cakes for two people.

a. How much of each ingredient would you need to make currant cakes for three people?

____

____

b. How much of each ingredient would you need to make currant cakes for five people?

____

____

Currant cakes for two people
2 eggs
120g butter
220g flour
120g currants
60g sugar
60ml milk

2. Answer the following questions for the cake recipe for five people.

a. I have only three eggs. How many more will I need? ________________

b. I have 325g of butter. How much will I have left? ________________

c. I have 300g of flour. How much more do I need? ________________

d. I have 180g of currants. How much more do I need? ________________

e. I have a quarter of a litre of milk. How much will I have left? ________________

School travel plan

One way of expressing an amount as a percentage of another amount is to first write it as a fraction, and then multiply by 100. So if 105 children out of 250 walk to school this can be written as $\frac{105}{250}$. Simplify the fraction to $\frac{21}{50}$ and then multiply by 100:

$\frac{21}{50} \times \frac{100}{1} = \frac{2100}{50} = \frac{210}{5} = 42\%$

There are 280 children in Central School. They have been conducting a survey for their travel plan to find out how children come to school. The table shows what they found out.

Walk to school	112
Come by car	98
By bike	70

1. What percentage of the children walk?

____

2. What percentage come by car?

____

3. What percentage cycle?

____

4. If 25% more children start walking to school by the end of the year, how many will now be walking?

____

All in a day

Proportions can be expressed as fractions. If you are looking at the proportion of time spent on an activity during 24 hours, each proportion can be written as a fraction of 24, for example $\frac{8}{24}$ hours sleeping. This can be simplified to $\frac{1}{3}$ of the day sleeping.

Have you ever wondered how you spend your time each day? Let's find out!

1. First of all, on a separate sheet of paper, list all of the activities you do during a school day, e.g. eating, travelling, sleeping and so on. Estimate how long you spend on each one.
2. Keep a log of everything you actually do during a day, For example 15 minutes eating, 30 minutes playing football, 1 hour watching television, 20 minutes eating and so on. The next morning, write down how long you were asleep.
3. Add up all the time you spent on each activity and round the result up or down to the nearest hour, For example 10 minutes for breakfast + 20 minutes for lunch + 20 minutes for tea = 50 minutes, rounded to the nearest hour = 1 hour eating. Make sure all of your activities add up to 24 hours.
4. Now fill in the table below, writing each activity as a proportion of the day, for example 2 hours spent playing would be $\frac{2}{24}$ or $\frac{1}{12}$.

Activity	Number of hours	Proportions

Compare these results to your estimates. Were there any surprises? Did you spend longer on something than you thought?

Scale up

Finding actual distances will involve multiplying, while finding map distances will involve dividing. Remember, the area of a rectangle = length × width. Wherever possible, ratios should be given in their lowest terms.

1. The scale of this map is 1cm to 5km.

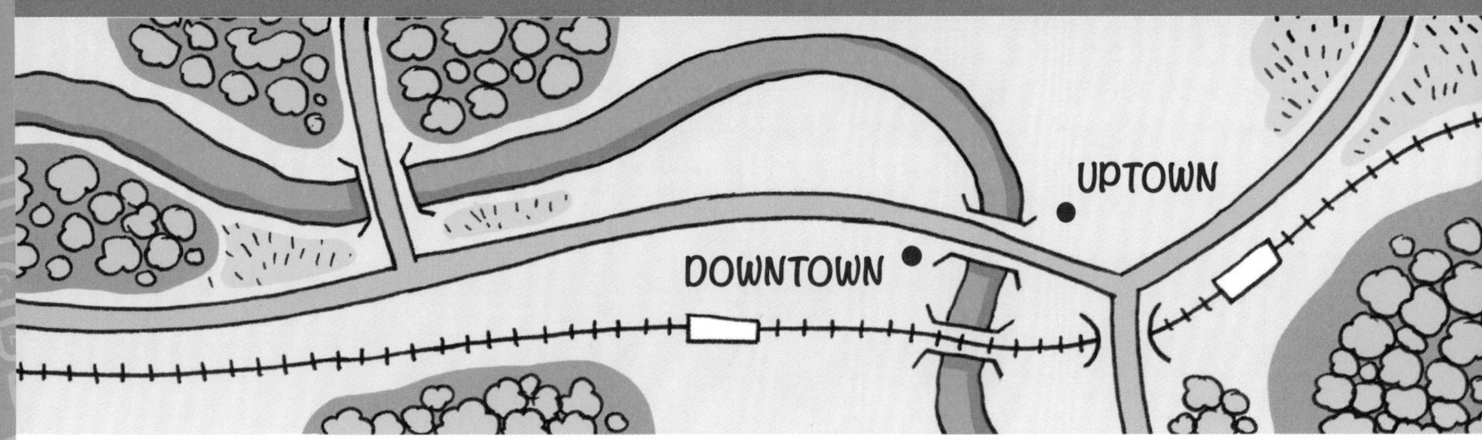

a. The distance from Downtown to Uptown on the map measures 2.2cm. What is the actual distance between the two towns?

____

b. Northtown is 9km north of Downtown. What should the distance between Northtown and Downtown be on the map?

____

c. Mark the position of Northtown on the map.

2. A rectangular tile design measures 2.5m × 3m. The pattern is reproduced for a floor with the length and breadth increased in the proportion 4:1.

a. What will the actual measurements of the floor pattern be?

____

b. What will the ratio of the area of the floor be to the area of the design?

____

Playground scale drawing

You have the opportunity to design your own dream playground. You must include a hard play area and a grass area, but the rest is up to you; you could add seating area, activity area with equipment and so on.

1. Draw a plan of your playground, showing measurements. Think about the scale for your plan, and write it below. Provide a key for your plan.

Scale: ______________________ Key: ______________________

2. When you have completed your design, calculate the area of grass and the area of hard play surface.

Area of grass: __________________ Area of hard play surface: __________________

Dinner arrangements

Remember, to find a percentage of an amount, divide the top by the bottom and then multiply by 100.

Always remember that where possible fraction calculations should be given in their lowest terms. Look to cancel down where you can.

There are 25 children in Class 5: 10 boys and 15 girls. Three girls and four boys have school dinners; the rest have packed lunch.

1. What percentage of the class are girls? ____________________

2. What fraction of the class bring packed lunch? ____________________

3. What percentage of the boys have school dinners? ____________________

4. What fraction of the girls have school dinners? ____________________

What's it worth?

Algebra is a branch of mathematics where letters are used in place of missing numbers. In algebra, if a letter or letters are next to each other, they must be multiplied not added. So 5x when x = 3 is 15.

Some answers may be worked out mentally but others will require jottings or written calculations.

Work out the value of each bauble on the tree. The value of each letter is given below.

a = 4 b = 3 c = 7 d = 5 e = 9

Express it!

Remember, expressions should be kept as brief as possible using only letters, numbers and operation signs.

To find the formula for the nth term in a sequence, look at what happens to each term in the sequence and write the rule, 1st 2nd 3rd 4th
5 10 15 20, each term is multiplied by 5.

So the rule for finding the nth term is 5n.

1. Write each of the statements below as a simple expression.

a. 9 sweets at n pence each: ____________________

b. The number of months in y years: ____________________

c. The formula for the area of a rectangle: ______________________________

d. The formula for finding the nth term of the sequence: 6, 12, 18, 24: ____________________

e. n marbles shared between 7 children: ____________________

2. Find the value of each equation if a = 4, b = 6, c = 5, d = 8 and e = 10.

a. bc ______________________________

b. a^2 ______________________________

c. 5e ______________________________

d. $45 - c^2$ ______________________________

e. cd + ae ______________________________

f. $3e^2$ ______________________________

g. $\frac{e}{c}$ ______________________________

Algy and Brian

Substitute the letters for numbers as you work through the problem. Notice that the formula remains the same throughout even when the values of either a or b are changed.

Algy and Brian each represent a different number.

- Algy = a and Brian = b.
- Algy is the number 26.
- $2a = 2b + a$

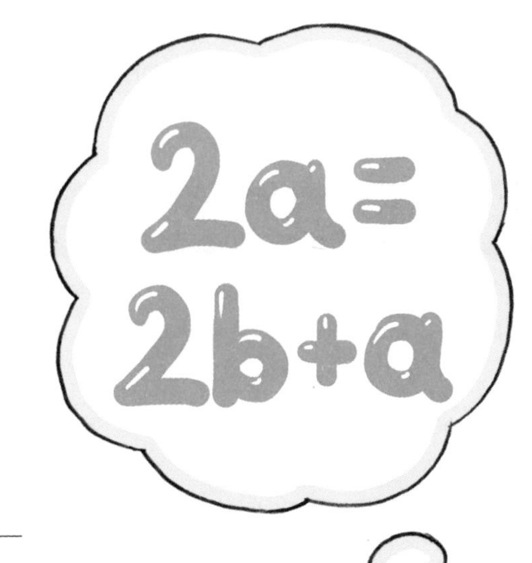

1. How much is Brian worth?

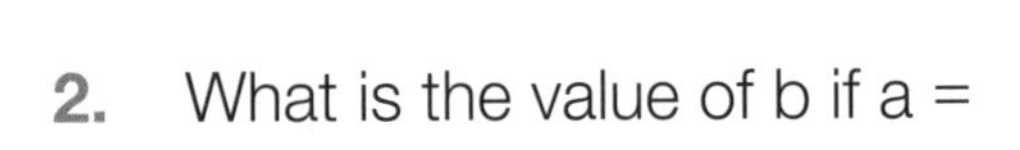

2. What is the value of b if a =

   a. 34? ______

   b. 102? ______

3. What is the value of a if b =

   a. 23? [ ]

   b. 54? [ ]

Letter time

Remember that in algebra, 4 × m is usually written as 4m and that where letters and numbers are written above others (such as $\frac{3n}{5}$) it means you should divide the number above the line by the number below the line.

1. If m = 10, n = 12, p = 6 and q = 5, find the values of the following statements.

a. $3q + 4 =$ ______________

b. $m + 5p =$ ______________

c. $12 + 3n =$ ______________

d. $n - 2q =$ ______________

e. $5q + m =$ ______________

f. $\frac{pq}{m} =$ ______________

g. $\frac{np}{6} =$ ______________

h. $\frac{qn}{p} =$ ______________

i. $p^2 - m - q =$ ______________

j. $(4q + 3p) - n =$ ______________

2. Solve these number sentences.

a. ▲ = 2 ■ + 1 What is the value of ▲ if:

■ = 1 ______________ ■ = 3 ______________ ■ = 5 ______________

■ = 2 ______________ ■ = 4 ______________

b. 2 ▲ = ■ + 2 What is the value of ▲ if:

■ = 2 ______________ ■ = 6 ______________ ■ = 10 ______________

■ = 4 ______________ ■ = 8 ______________

c. ▲ = 3 ■ − 1 What is the value of ▲ if:

■ = 1 ______________ ■ = 3 ______________ ■ = 5 ______________

■ = 2 ______________ ■ = 4 ______________

Equations with two unknowns

Where there are two unknowns in a number statement, there will be more than one answer to each problem. For $a + b = 10$ there are many solutions. For example $a = 1$ and $b = 9$ or $a = 2$ and $b = 8$ or $a = -3$ and $b = 13$.

1. Solve these equations in which there are two unknowns. There will be more than one answer for each question. Try to use as much variety as you can and try to use some negative numbers where possible.

a. $x + y = 15$ ________________________

b. $t - v = 12$ ________________________

c. $20 = s \times n$ ________________________

d. $p \div w = 3$ ________________________

e. $15 = x + 2y$ ________________________

f. $2x + y = 25$ ________________________

g. $2y - x = 1$ ________________________

h. $4x + 2y = 20$ ________________________

i. $y - 4x = 7$ ________________________

j. $8x - 2y = 34$ ________________________

k. $48 = 4b \times 2c$ ________________________

l. $6x + y = -1$ ________________________

Finding other unknowns

You will need to know certain mathematical rules to solve some problems. For example, to find the sum of the angles of a triangle is always 180 degrees and the sum of the angles of a quadrilateral is always 360 degrees. You will also need to know how to read coordinates and have knowledge of the properties of certain 2D shapes.

1. Find the missing angles marked with a letter in these shapes.

a.

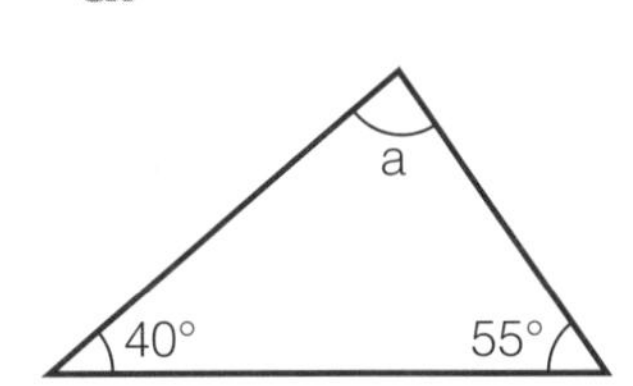

b.

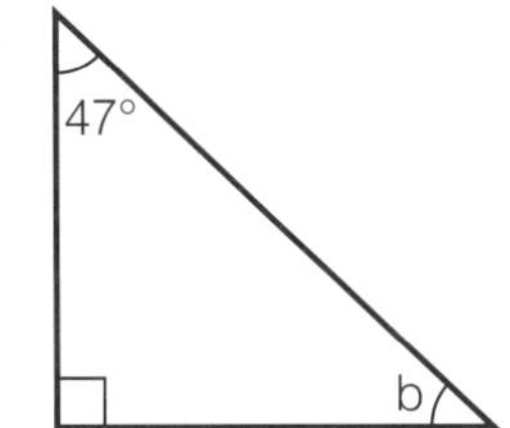

c.

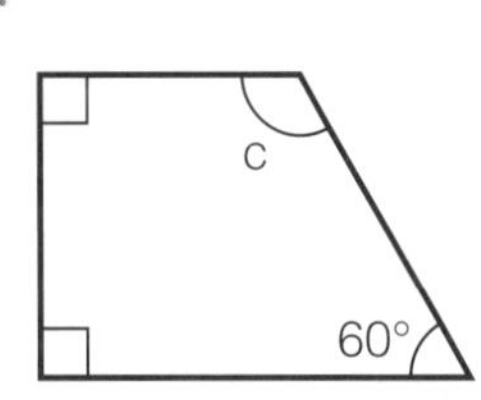

d.

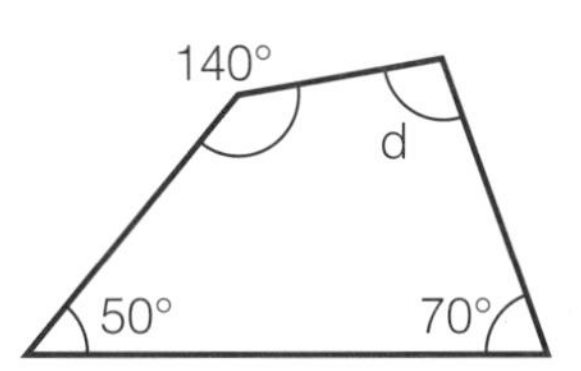

2. Give the coordinates for the points a, b, c and d.

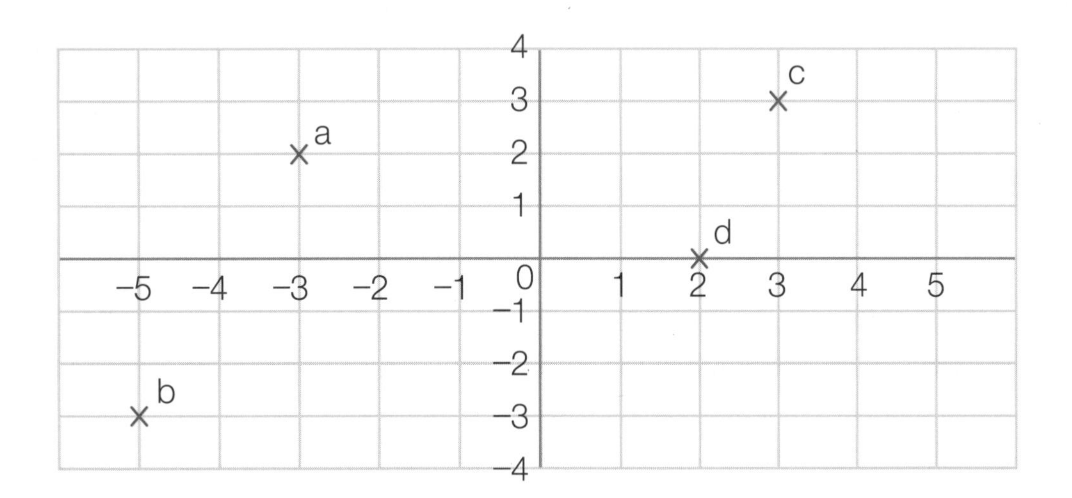

3. Find the length of each side marked with a letter in these shapes.

a.

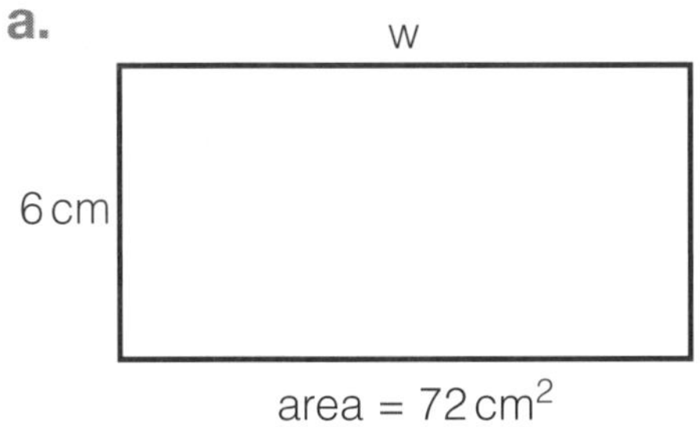

w = __________

b.

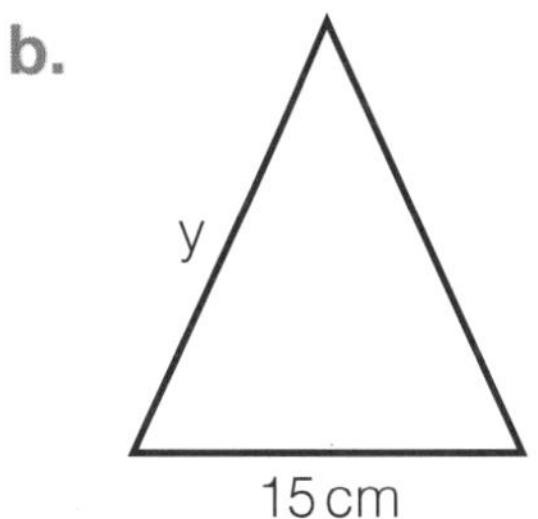

y = __________

What's next?

Sequences do not always increase by the same interval each time. For example, the sequence +2, +4, +6 would give a pattern of 5, 7, 11, 17 and so on.

Some sequences may have two operations in each step, such as ×2, −1 as in the pattern 10, 20, 21, 42, 43 and so on.

1. Look carefully at each sequence. For each one, write down the next three numbers or letters in the sequence and explain the rule.

a. 17 22 28 35 ☐ ☐ ☐ The rule is ______________________

b. 98 50 26 ☐ ☐ ☐ The rule is ______________________

c. 25 36 49 ☐ ☐ ☐ The rule is ______________________

d. $\frac{1}{4}$ $\frac{2}{8}$ $\frac{4}{16}$ ☐ ☐ ☐ The rule is ______________________

e. A D H ☐ ☐ ☐ The rule is ______________________

f. 2 7 22 67 ☐ ☐ ☐ The rule is ______________________

2. Now write three sequences of your own and explain the rule for each.

a. ☐ ☐ ☐ ☐ ☐ ☐

The rule is ______________________

b. ☐ ☐ ☐ ☐ ☐ ☐

The rule is ______________________

c. ☐ ☐ ☐ ☐ ☐ ☐

The rule is ______________________

Jumping frog number patterns

For sequences that follow two-step rules, work from the known to the unknown – work out what the rule is and then use it to predict what numbers will follow as the sequence continues. You can always jot down what is happening in the sequence in the gaps between numbers.

Imagine you own a jumping frog that only jumps in a regular pattern.

Today he is jumping a small jump followed by a larger jump. He lands on the numbers 0, 2, 5, 7, 10 and 12.

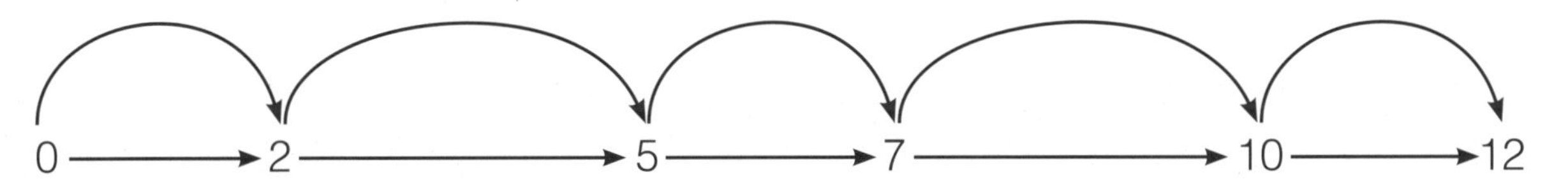

1. What is the jumping rule? What are the next four numbers that your frog will land on?

____

2. Sometimes your frog jumps differently. Find the rule and the next four numbers your frog will land on if it jumps in these sequences.

a. 0 → 4 → 7 → 11 → 14 ______________________________

b. 0 → 6 → 9 → 15 → 18 ______________________________

c. 0 → 7 → 12 → 19 → 24 ______________________________

Your frog can also jump backwards.

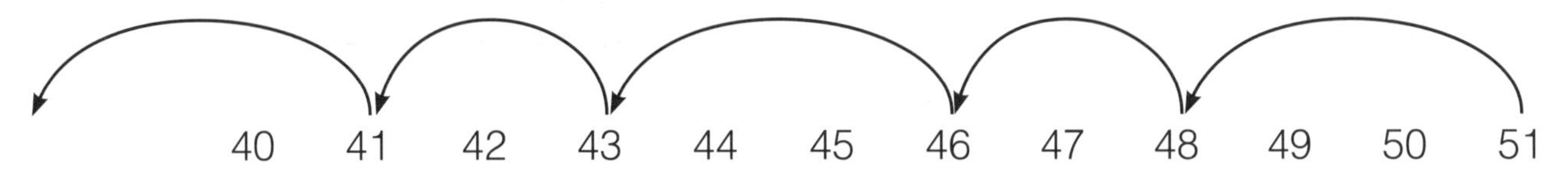

3. What is the number sequence now? What are the next four numbers?

____

In sequence

You may find it useful to explain the rules of a number sequence to someone verbally before writing it down.

1. Give the next four numbers in these sequences. Write the pattern used at the end.

a. 0 5 9 15 18 ______________________

b. 0 2 8 10 16 ______________________

c. 3 5.5 8 10.5 13 ______________________

2. Write in the missing numbers in each of these sequences. Explain the rule that has been used to make the sequence.

a. $\frac{23}{8}$ ______ $\frac{27}{8}$ ______ $\frac{33}{8}$ ______ $\frac{41}{8}$

Rule: ______________________

b. 0.15 0.8 ______ 2.1 ______ ______ 4.05 ______

Rule: ______________________

3. This pattern continues in the same way. Answer the questions.

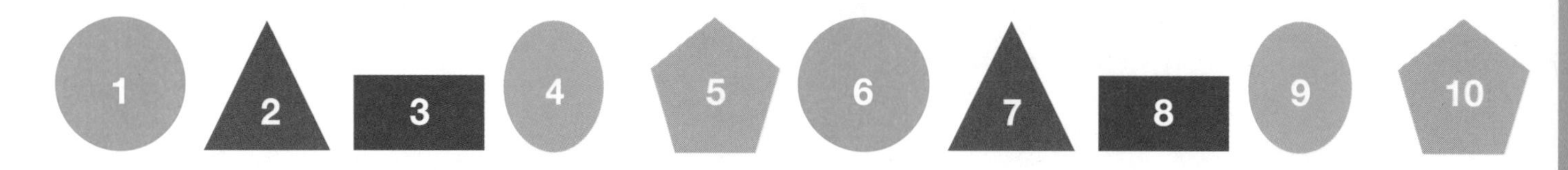

a. Which shape appears in the 28th position? ______________

b. How many triangles will there be until you reach the number 40? ______________

c. Explain how you found your answers. ______________________

____

Algebra problems

Expressions can be simplified by putting the terms together, for example h + h + h can be written as 3h and 5y + 3 + 4 – 2y can be written as 3y + 7. Expressions are also a shorthand way of writing longer number statements or sentences, for example 'Five less than a mystery number' can be written as x – 5.

1. Simplify the following expressions.

a. $f + f + f + f =$ ____________

b. $5 + n + 10 =$ ____________

c. $g + 6 + g - 8 =$ ____________

d. $2h + h + 3h - h =$ ____________

e. $g + g + g + h + h + h =$ ____________

f. $3x + 2y + 2x - y =$ ____________

2. The mystery number is x. Draw a line to match each description in words with the correct expression.

The mystery number multiplied by six and added to two.	$x + 3$
Two divided by the mystery number.	$50 \div x$
Three more than the mystery number.	$6x + 2$
The mystery number added to two then multiplied by six.	x^2
The mystery number divided by two.	$x \div 50$
The mystery number divided by fifty.	$2 \div x$
Fifty divided by the mystery number.	$x \div 2$
The mystery number multiplied by itself.	$6(x + 2)$

Estimating length

Make sensible choices when deciding what type of measuring devices you are going to use for each item you measure.

Remember that 10mm = 1cm and 100cm = 1m.

You are going to carry out some measurement tasks at home. You will need a 30cm ruler, a metre stick (or equivalent strip of paper) and a measuring tape.

1. Choose items suitable for the type of measuring device you are using (for example a book for the ruler, a shelf for the metre stick and the length of a room for the tape measure). Aim to measure two or three items with each device.
2. Before you measure each item, estimate how long you think it will be and write down your estimate. When measuring each item, be accurate to the nearest millimetre. If this proves difficult, round to the nearest half-centimetre.
3. Finally, write down the measurements in at least one other way (for example 7cm 8mm could be written as 78mm, 94cm could be written as 0.94m and 5m 17cm could be written as 517cm).

Item measured	Estimate	Measurement	Second recording

Ordering lengths

Ordering lengths is difficult unless you put each of the measurements being considered into the same unit, such as millimetres, centimetres or metres. For example, 3cm 2mm and 4.7cm could be written as 32mm and 47mm.

1. Place these lengths in order of size, smallest first.

90mm 7cm 8mm 6.5cm 48mm 9.8cm 4cm 3mm

____

____

2. Place these heights in order of size, largest first.

1.75m 106cm 1m 32cm 1m 58cm 141cm 1.09m

____

____

3. Place these distances in order, smallest first.

4.75km 3900m 6km 200m 4km 86m 5.002km 8003m

____

____

Estimating mass

You are going to carry out some measurement tasks. You will need kitchen scales and various objects to weigh. Make sure you ask permission before using anything.

1. Choose a range of objects that will give quite different weights, and spend some time checking you can read information on the scales before weighing. First estimate the weight of each object.
2. Weigh each object to see how accurate your estimate was.
3. Record your information in the chart below, writing the weights in three different ways. Remember: 1250g = 1.25kg = 1kg 250g.

Object	Estimate	Actual weight		
		g	kg	kg and g

Liquid measures

For liquid measures, first check that you can read the information on the measuring cylinders by counting the small divisions between the 100ml marks. It may help to place a ruler across the cylinder or jug at the same level as the liquid.

1. How much liquid is shown on each of these scales?

A

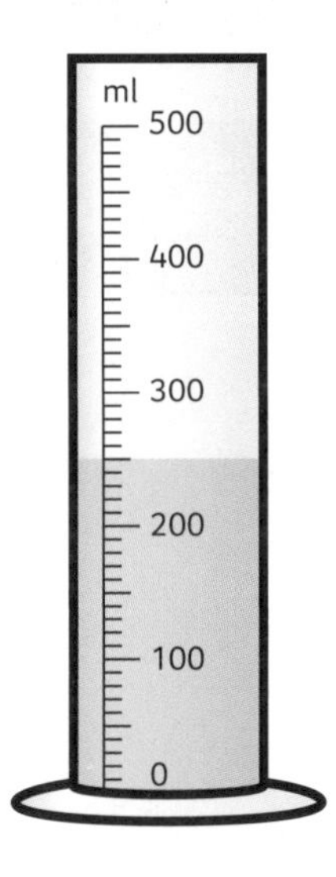

____

B

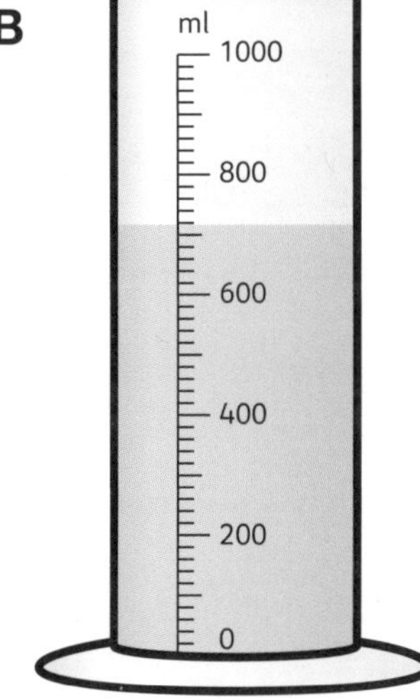

____

2. The volume of water is shown in two measuring jugs, X and Y.

a. Which jug contains more water?

____

b. How much more does it contain?

____

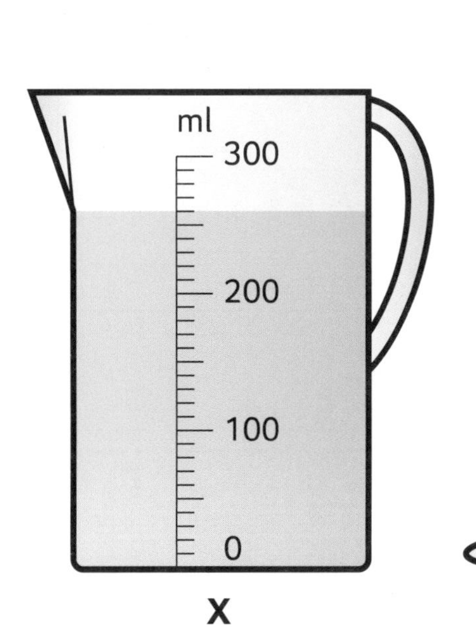

X

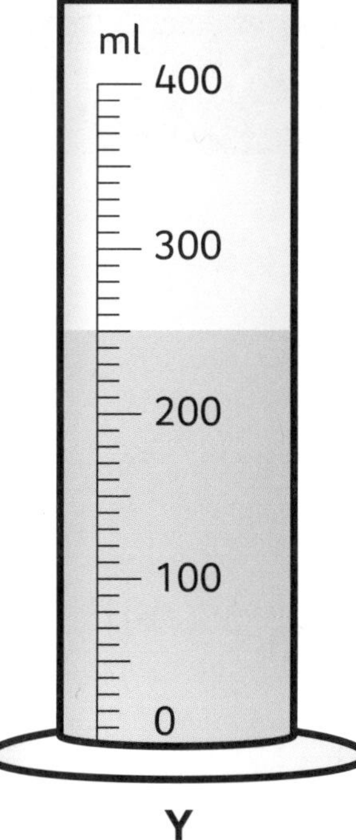

Y

Converting units of measures

The location of decimal points will be very important in the answers. There may be some metric units here that you are less familiar with. Note: 1000kg = 1 tonne and 1 centilitre (cl) = 10ml. So 3250kg = 3.250 tonne and 1750ml = 175cl.

Carry out the following conversions between metric units. You will need to use decimal numbers to give the answers.

1. Change from litres to centilitres.	**2. Change from centilitres to litres.**
a. 11.5 l ______	a. 175cl ______
b. 12.75 l ______	b. 215cl ______
c. 18.5 l ______	c. 870cl ______
d. 22.5 l ______	d. 1460cl ______
3. Change from kilograms to tonnes.	**4. Change from tonnes to kilograms.**
a. 1275kg ______	a. $4\frac{1}{2}$ tonnes ______
b. 3470kg ______	b. 5.9 tonnes ______
c. 5500kg ______	c. 12.35 tonnes ______
d. 12578kg ______	d. 10.43 tonnes ______

Converting and ordering units

Ordering cannot be done successfully until the given quantities are put into the same units. For example, to order 27g, 0.27kg, 0.027 tonne, change the units first: 0.027kg, 0.27kg, 27kg. Remember, 1000kg = 1 tonne and 1cl = 10ml.

1. Put each of these sets of masses in order of size, smallest first.

a.	426g	0.47kg	0.046 tonne	4kg 250g	47g
	______	______	______	______	______
b.	550g	0.005 tonne	1.54kg	5kg 50g	5005g
	______	______	______	______	______
c.	650g	0.06 tonne	0.75kg	1.35kg	3kg 450g
	______	______	______	______	______

2. Put each of these sets of capacities in order of size, largest first.

a.	0.04 l	304ml	35cl	3 l 570ml	1.7 l
	______	______	______	______	______
b.	1.23 l	2 l 310ml	315cl	3.2 l	2131ml
	______	______	______	______	______
c.	4.6 l	640ml	65cl	6 l 400ml	4060ml
	______	______	______	______	______

Happy hundred!

Leap years have 366 days instead of 365. They happen every 4 years. We know which they are as they divide by 4 exactly, 2008, 2012, 2016. We only count centennial years as leap years if the first two digits divide exactly by 4, 1600 and 2000 but not 1800 and 1900.

Jeanne Calment from France is thought to have been the world's oldest living person. She lived until she was 122 years old!

- How many days is it until your 100th birthday? Use the box below to work out your answer, then write it here. ____________________

Tip: don't forget leap years! (2012 was a leap year)

- Can you find out what day your 100th birthday will be on? Show how you worked it out.

  I will be celebrating my 100th birthday on a ____________________.

How long?

1. Emma wants to find out how much walking she does each day. She keeps a time log to help her. Fill in the gaps.

Journey	Time started	Time finished	Time taken
Home to school	8.10am	8.35am	
School to home	3.15pm		25 minutes
To friend's house		4.18pm	23 minutes
To the swimming pool		6.40pm	35 minutes

2. Pat the lorry driver has to complete a table of his journeys to give to his boss. How long did each journey take? Complete the table. Work in units of 60 as 60 minutes = 1 hour.

Journey	Time started	Time finished	Time taken
Day 1	9.05am	1.55pm	
Day 2	10.20am	3.10pm	
Day 3	4.45pm	11.20pm	
Day 4	8.25pm	2.05am	
Day 5			

3. On Day 5, he leaves the depot at 11.35am. His journey takes 6 hours 15 minutes. What time does he arrive at his destination? Complete the table.

Moon traveller

The moon is approximately 384,000km from Earth.
Five miles is approximately eight kilometres.

1. Approximately how many miles are there between the Moon and Earth? ______________

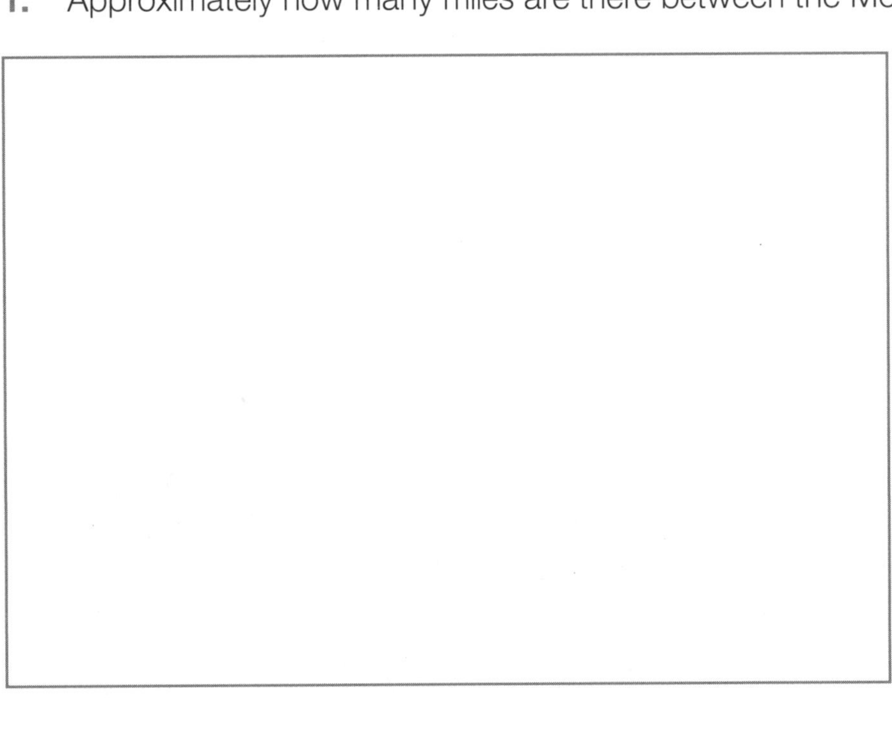

This approximation 5 miles = 8km is the same as 1.6km = 1 mile.

2. Use the same conversion to work out the following distances. You may need to round off the distances you choose to make the figures easier to work with.

Distance	Kilometres	Miles
The distance from your home to school and back again.		
The distance you went on your last holiday (one way).		
How far you travelled, in total, last weekend.		

Converting miles to kilometres and vice versa

Remember, the graph must start from zero as no distance has been travelled at this point. If each point is plotted accurately, the graph will form a straight line because the distances increase by the same amount each time. This is known in maths as constant proportion.

1. Mark these distances on the grid to make a straight line graph converting miles into kilometres and vice versa.

Miles	10	20	30	40	50	60	70	80
Kilometres	16	32	48	64	80	96	112	128

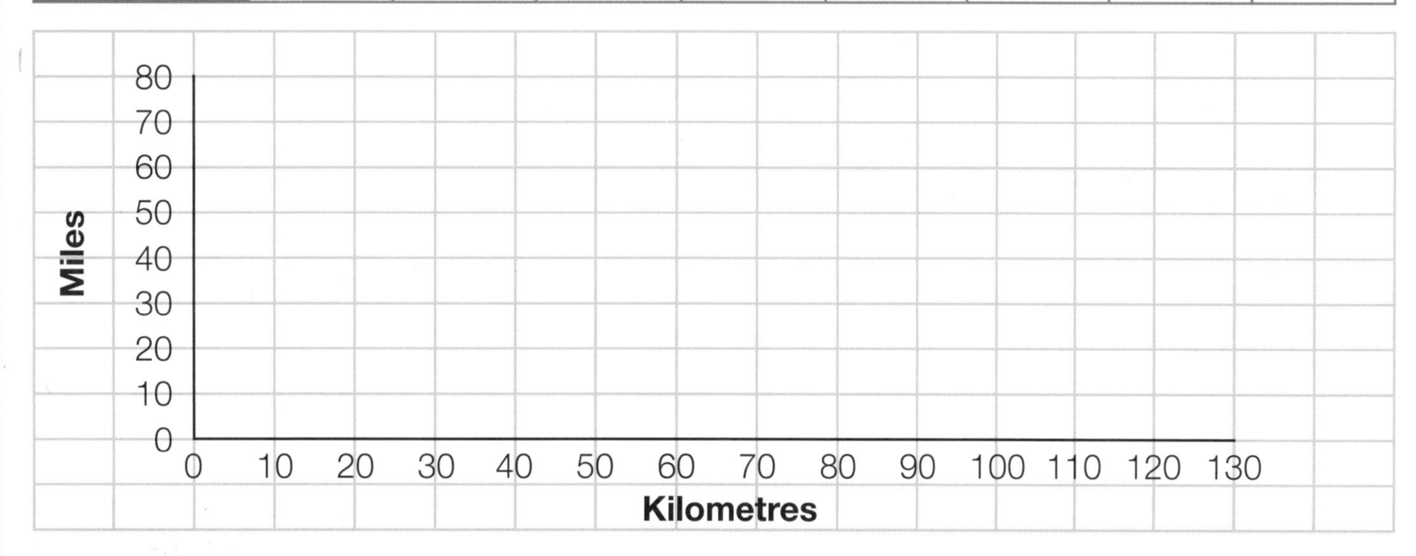

2. Convert these distances to kilometres.

a. 20 miles ______ b. 30 miles ______ c. 50 miles ______

d. 15 miles ______ e. 25 miles ______ f. 45 miles ______

3. Convert these distances to miles.

a. 40km ______ b. 60km ______ c. 20km ______

d. 15km ______ e. 55km ______ f. 75km ______

Same area, different perimeter

Remember, area concerns surface covered, while perimeter is the distance around the outside or edge of a shape. Think of efficient ways to find a perimeter rather than counting squares, such as width + length × 2.

1. Mr Fixit has to build a new patio in the garden of The Crossed Forks restaurant. He has 60 one-metre-square patio slabs. What different rectangular patios can he make with his slabs? Which arrangement gives the biggest perimeter? Record your findings in this chart.

Length	Width	Perimeter

Biggest perimeter: ______________________

2. The restaurant owners have decided not to have a rectangular patio. Use the squared paper below to find the compound shape (made up of small squares) that will give the greatest perimeter. The patio slabs must fit together side by side – they cannot overlap or join together with just the corners touching. What is the biggest perimeter you can find?

Biggest perimeter: ______________________

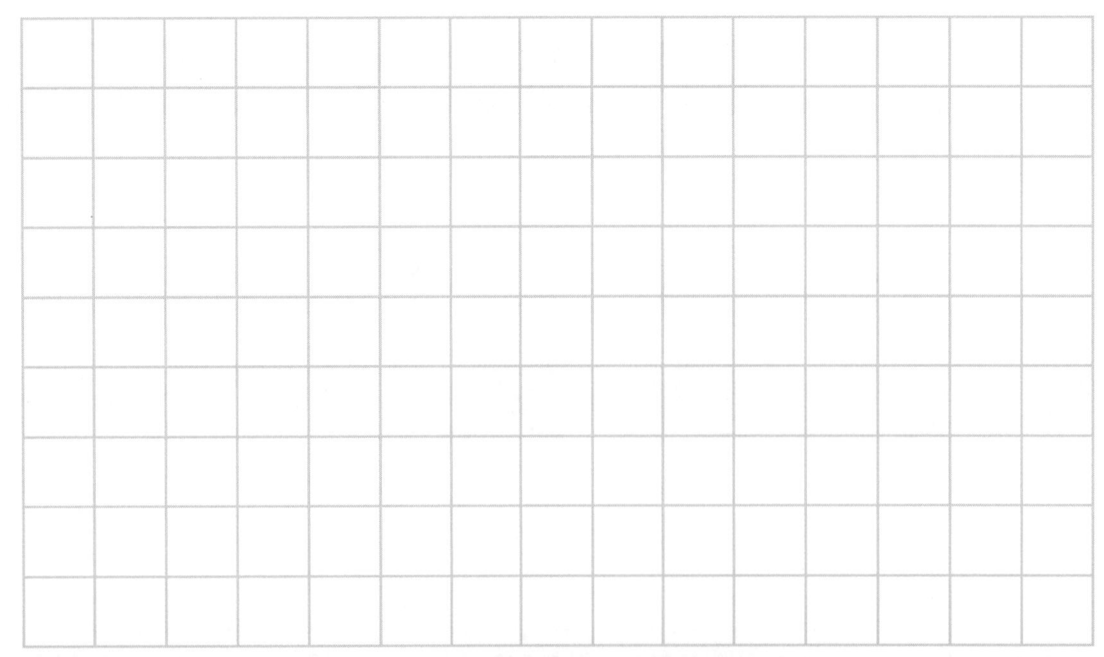

All square

Squaring a number means multiplying it by itself. So 5 squared, which can be written 5^2, is 5 × 5 = 25. Use number facts to help you with larger numbers. if 8 × 8 = 64 then 80 × 8 = 640, 80 × 80 = 6400 and 800 × 80 = 64,000.

1. Write down the squares of numbers to 12 × 12 in the space below.

2. Now use your knowledge of square numbers to help you work out the answers to these problems.

a. How much material will I need to cover both sides of a piece of cardboard measuring 40cm by 40cm?

____

b. Mr Smith has a vegetable plot that measures 900cm by 900cm. He builds a square water tank in the middle of the plot that measures 200cm by 200cm. How much space has he got left to grow vegetables?

____

c. Mrs Smith is buying a new carpet for her bedroom. Her bedroom measures 11m by 11m. The carpet costs £7 a square metre. How much does she pay?

____

d. Mr Singh is sowing new grass seed on the local playing field. The field measures 120m by 120m. It takes him one minute to sow 10 square metres. How many minutes will it take him to sow the whole field?

____

Areas of rooms

Remember that area concerns the surface of a shape while perimeter is the distance around it. You can split compound shapes into convenient rectangles and squares and use the formula for finding the area of a rectangle or square: area = length × width.

The Johnson family is moving house. Sarah Johnson has been looking at details of some of the houses they have been to see because she wants to have the largest bedroom possible.

1. The measurements of the rooms she has seen so far are given below. Work out the floor area of each one to find out which will provide the most space. Write the area in the middle of each shape.

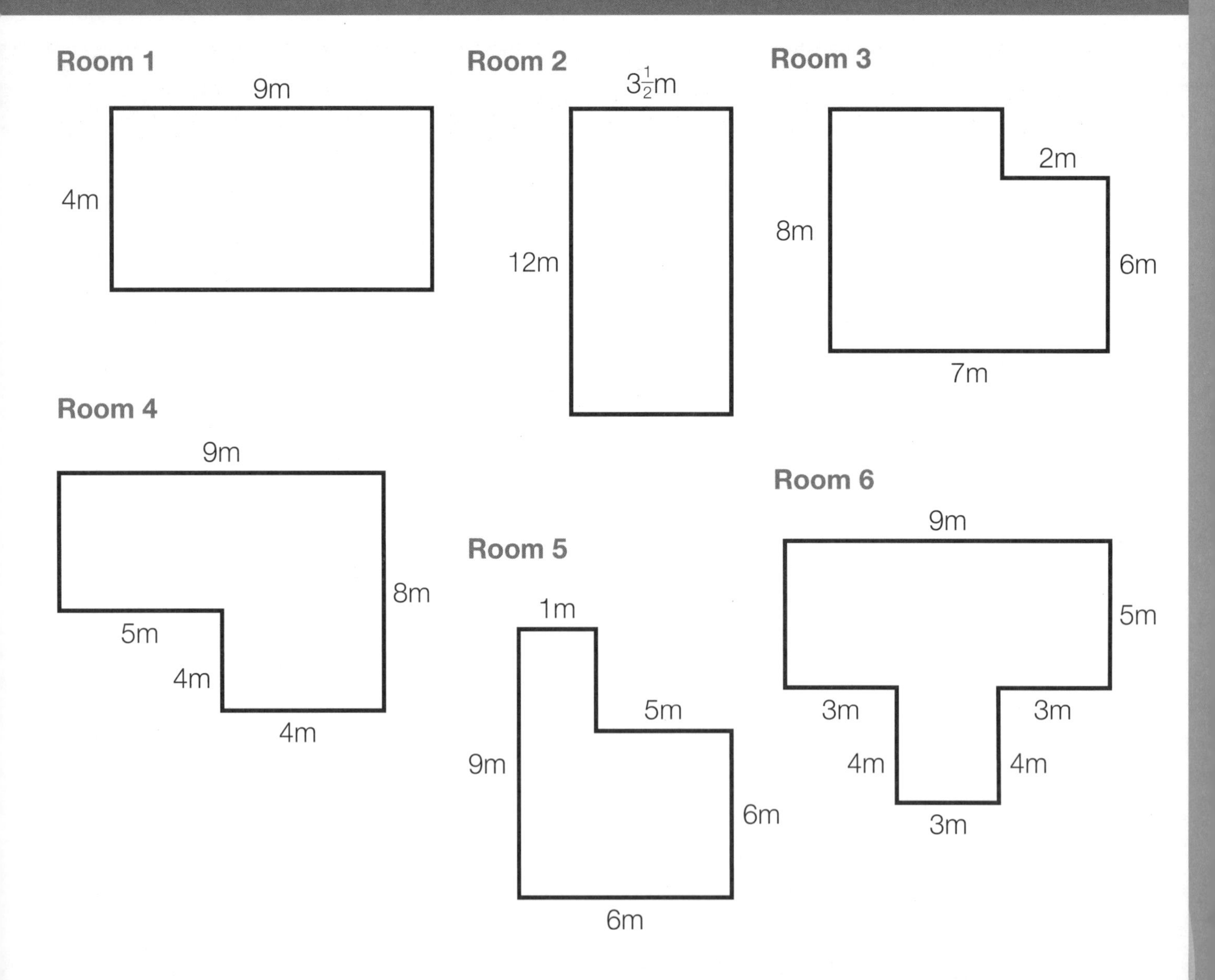

Areas of parallelograms and triangles

To find the amount of surface in a shape, you can split parallelograms into convenient rectangles and triangles.

The formula for finding the area of a triangle is $\frac{1}{2}$ base × height or base × height ÷ 2.

1. Find the areas of these triangles.

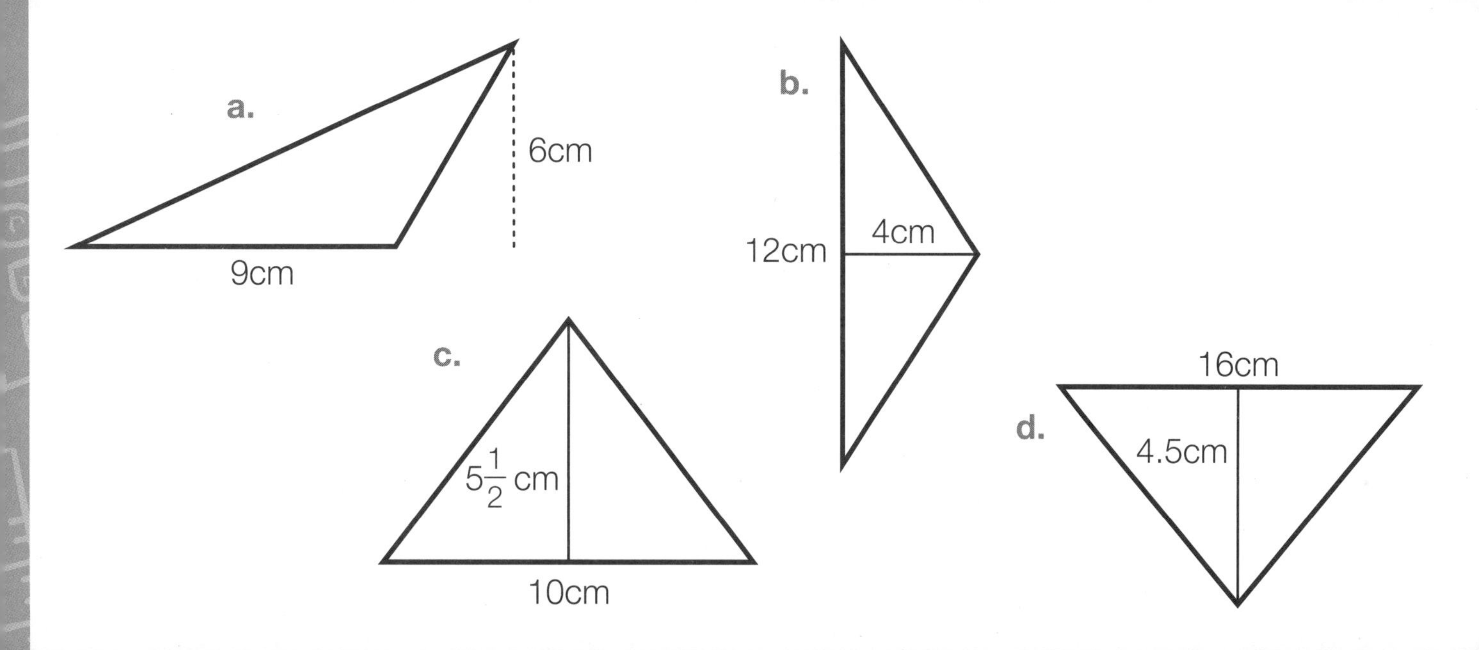

2. Find the area of these parallelograms.

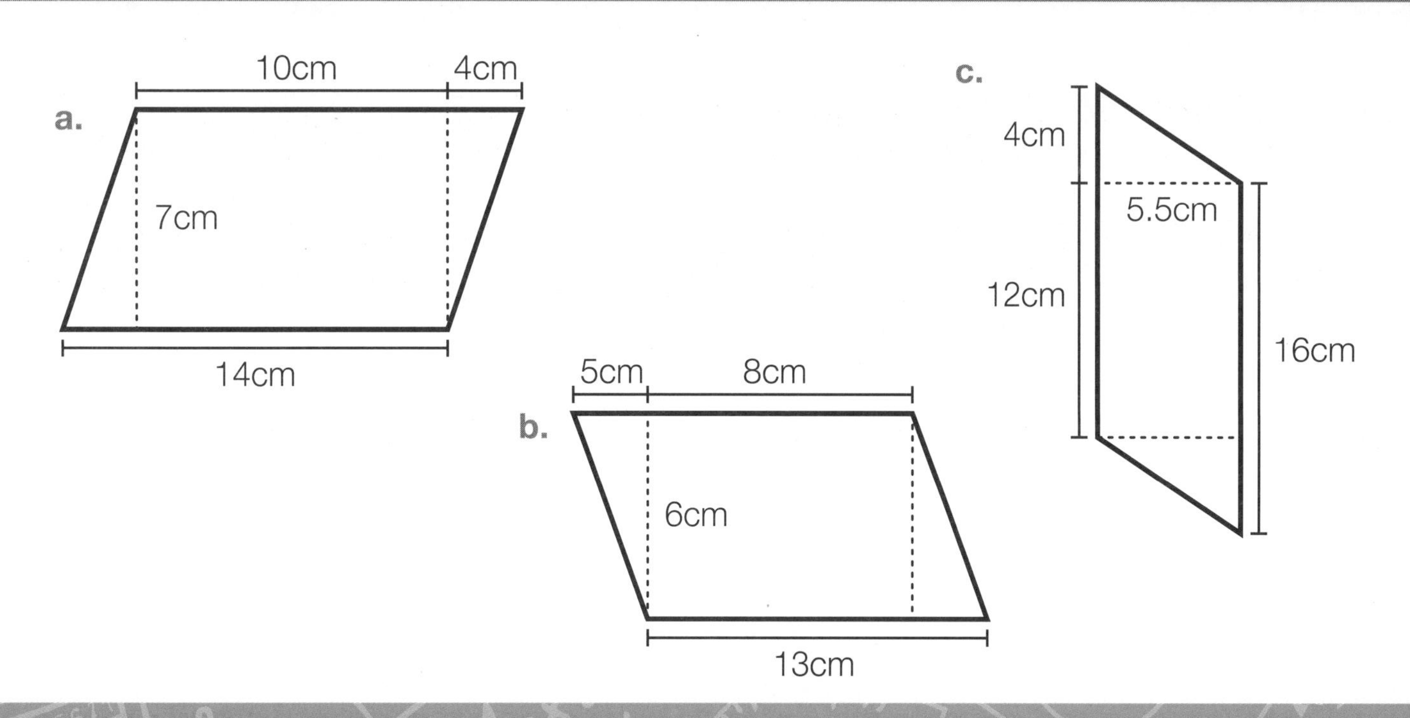

Volumes of cubes and cuboids

The volume of 3D shapes is measured in cubic millimetres (mm^3), cubic centimetres (cm^3) and cubic metres (m^3).
The formula for finding the volume of a cube or cuboid is length × width × height.

1. Find the volume of these cubes and cuboids.

a.

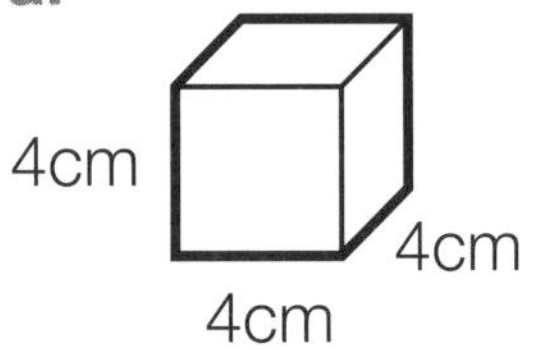

b.

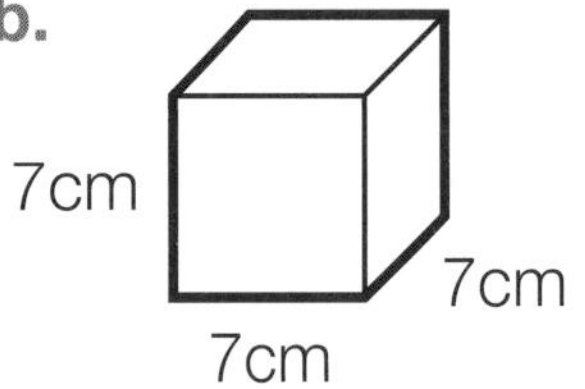

c.

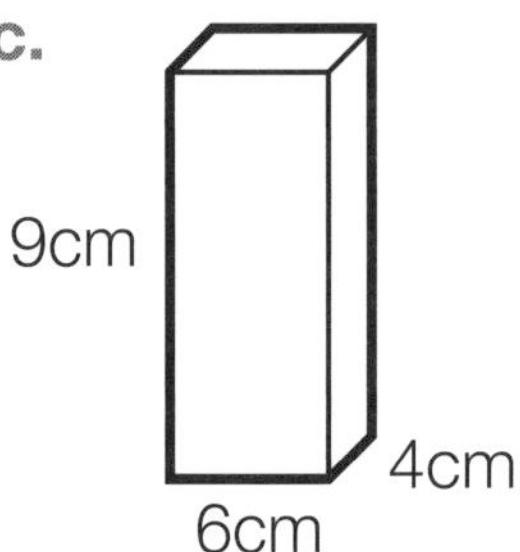

d.

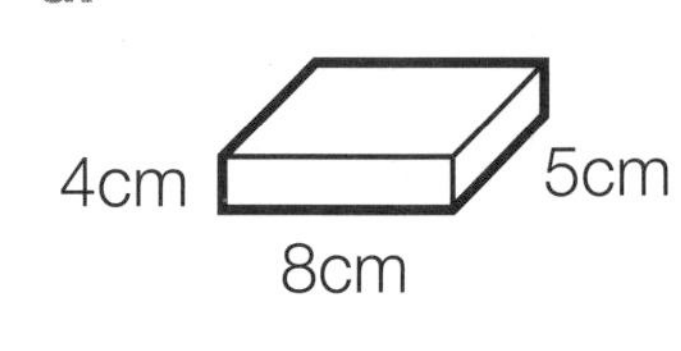

a. ______________________

b. ______________________

c. ______________________

d. ______________________

e. ______________________

f. ______________________

e.

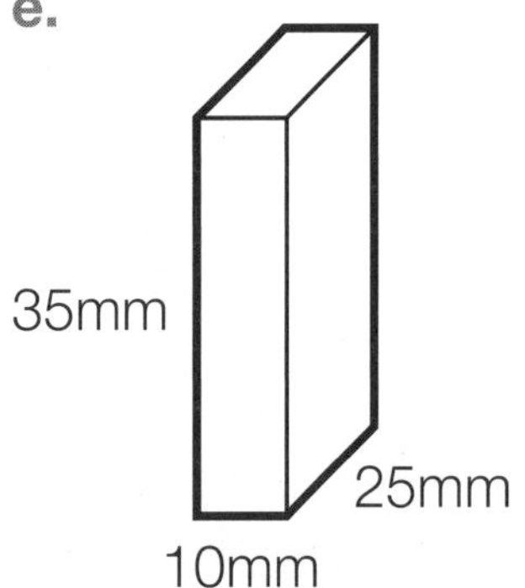

f.

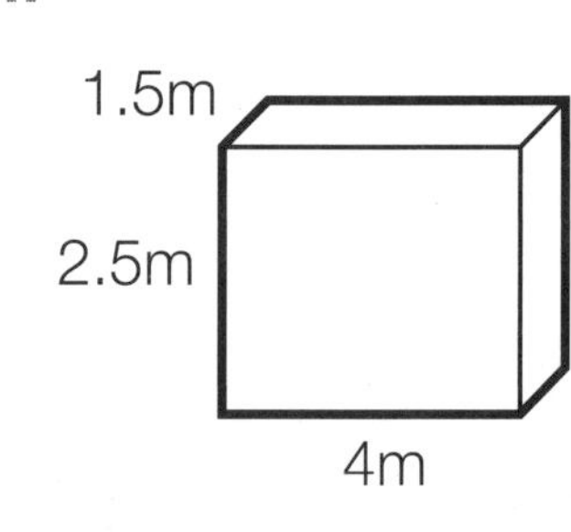

2. This table shows the sizes of some cuboids. Fill in the gap.

Length (cm)	Width (cm)	Height (cm)	Volume (cm^3)
4cm	5cm	6cm	
	3cm	4cm	$24cm^3$
4cm		10cm	$80cm^3$
3cm	3cm		$117cm^3$

3. Which of these cuboids have the same volume?

a.

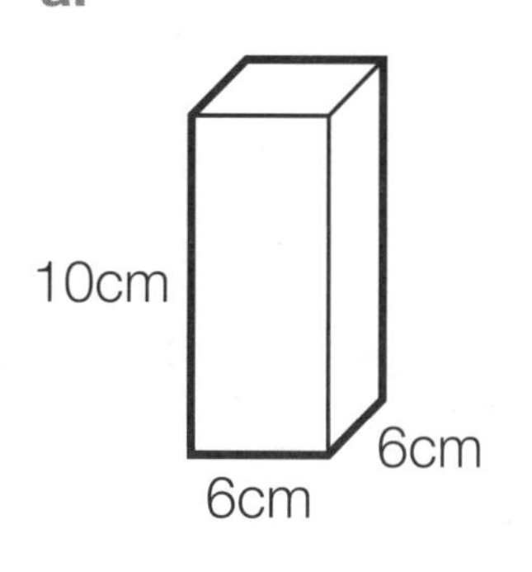

b.

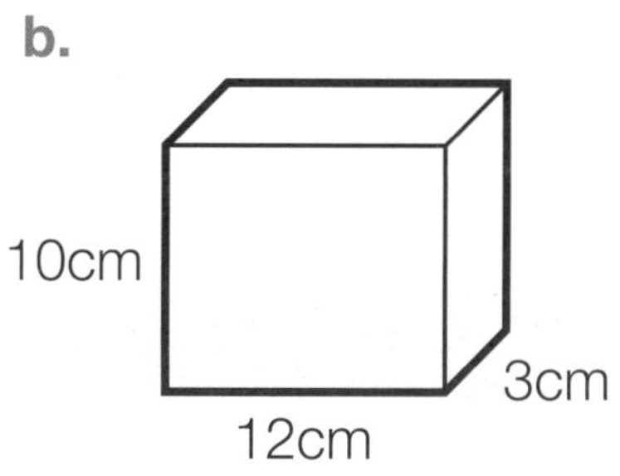

c.

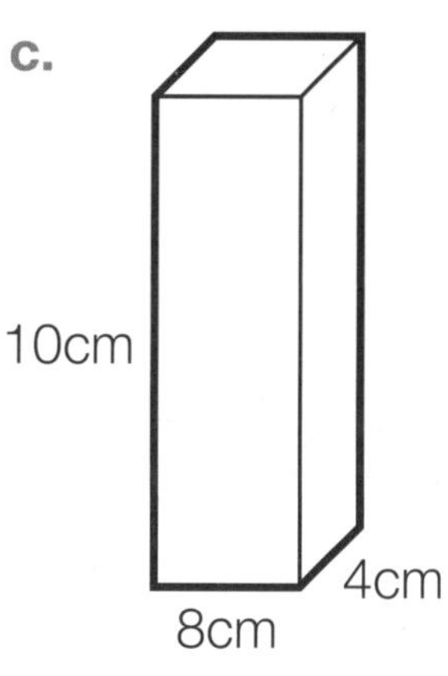

d.

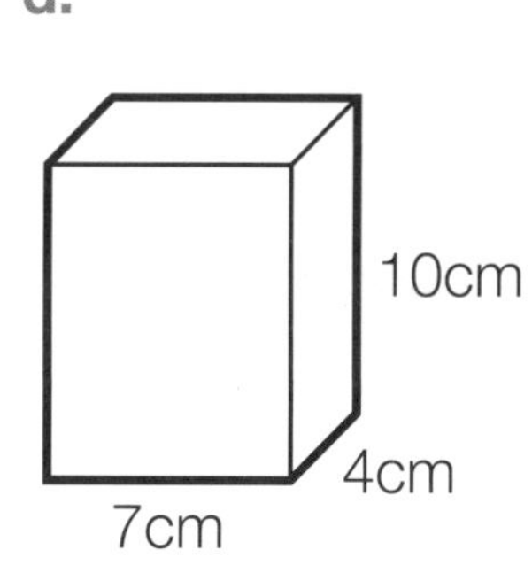

a. ______________ b. ______________ c. ______________ d. ______________

4. Which of these boxes has the greatest volume? Write an estimate first.

a.

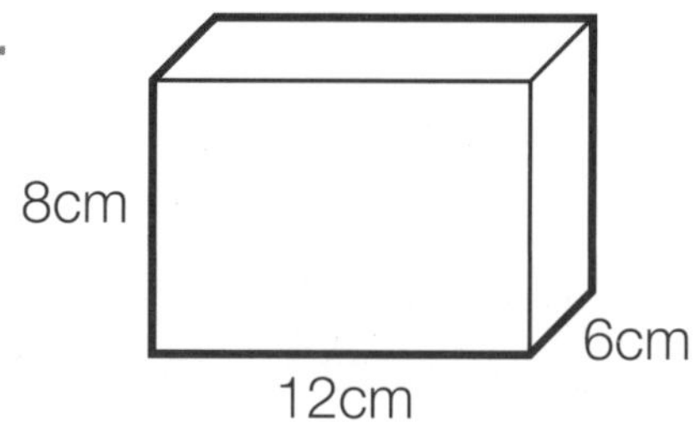

Estimate ______________________________

Greatest volume ______________________________

b.

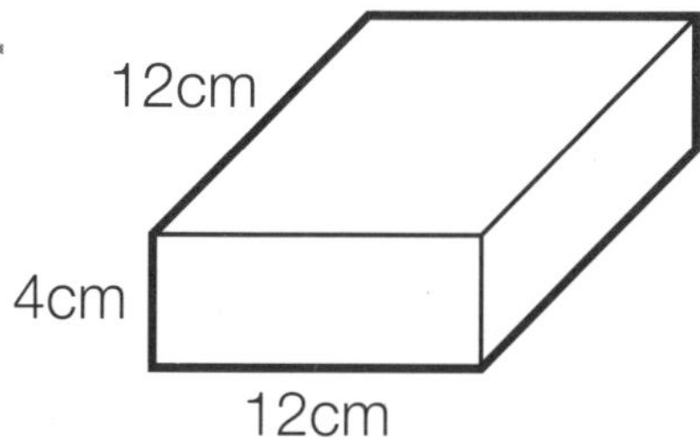

Estimate ______________________________

Greatest volume ______________________________

c.

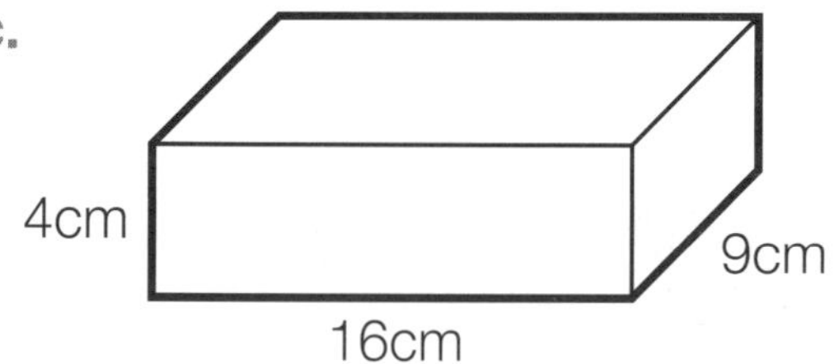

Estimate ______________________________

Greatest volume ______________________________

Circles

When drawing circles, you should use a ruler to set the compass to the radius length.

There are important relationships between circle parts to learn, especially between radius and diameter and diameter and circumference.

1. Label the three parts of the circle shown.

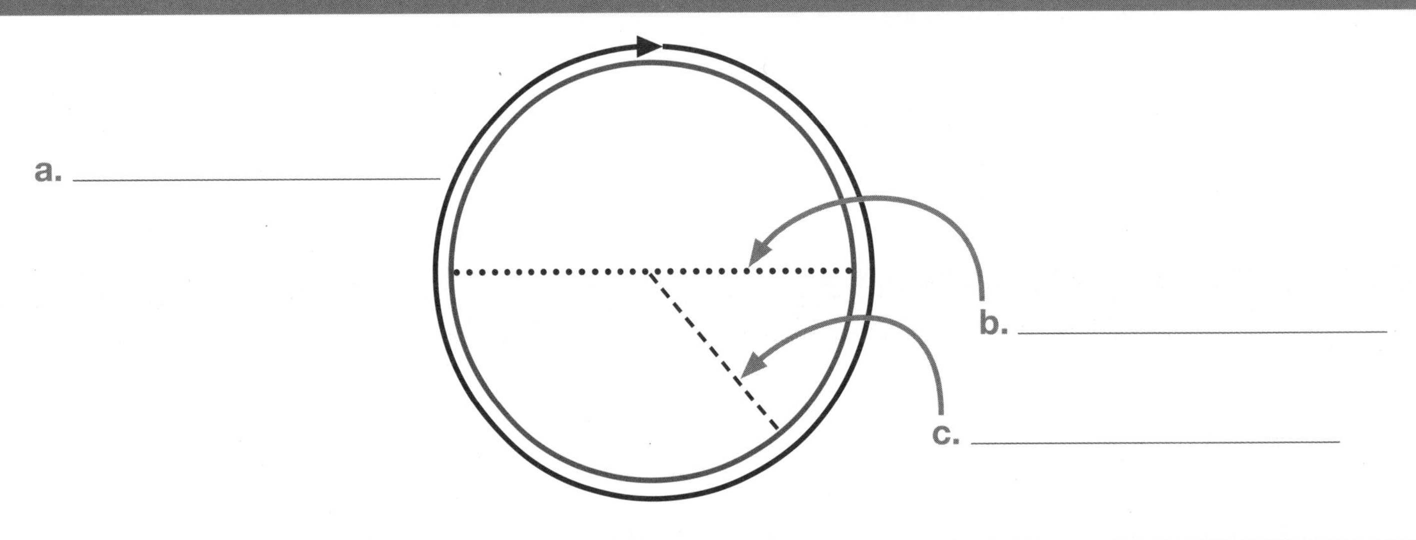

2. Draw circles with the following diameter measurement. The circles can overlap.

a. 4cm b. 1.5cm c. 3.5cm

3. Measure the radius and the diameter of each circle. What do you notice about the measurements in each case?

______

4. **Draw circles with the following radius measurement.**

a. 1cm b. 2cm c. 3cm

5. **Measure the diameter of each of these circles with a ruler. Then use a piece of string to measure the circumference as accurately as you can. What do you notice about the two measurements in each case?**

____

6. **Draw a large circle. Find out what the following circle words mean. Mark them on your circle.**

semicircle * quadrant * arc * chord * segment * sector

Measuring and drawing angles

A right angle is 90°. When you estimate an angle, think about how much bigger or smaller the angle is compared to a right angle. When you measure angles, make sure your protractor is positioned accurately and you are reading off the size of the angle on the correct scale.

1. Look carefully at each of these angles. Estimate the size of the angle, and then measure it carefully with a protractor.

a.

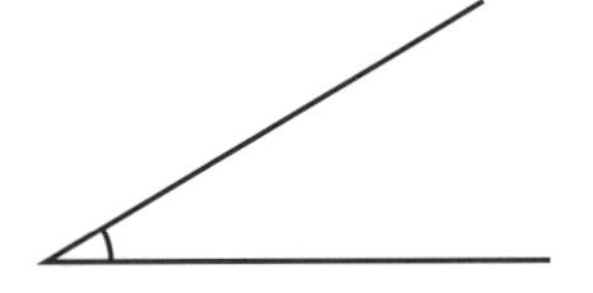

Estimate ________

Measurement ________

b.

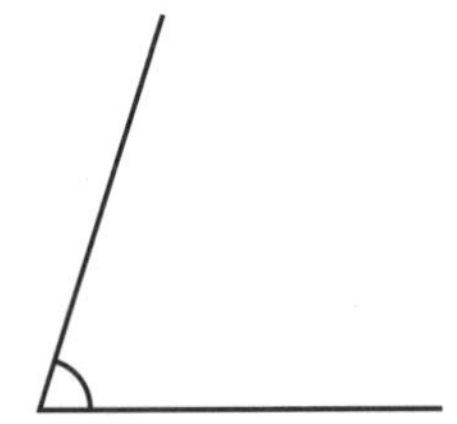

Estimate ________

Measurement ________

c.

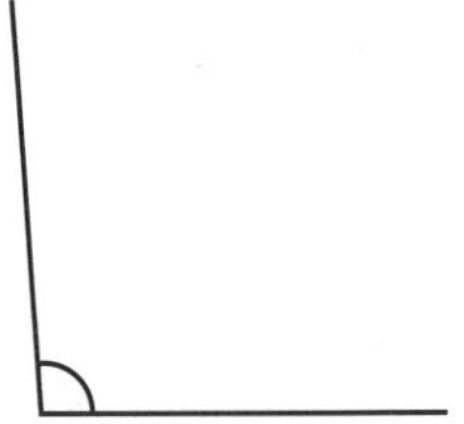

Estimate ________

Measurement ________

d.

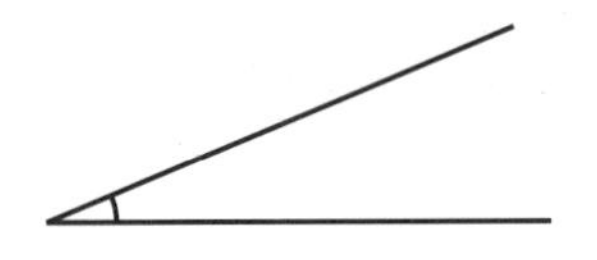

Estimate ________

Measurement ________

e.

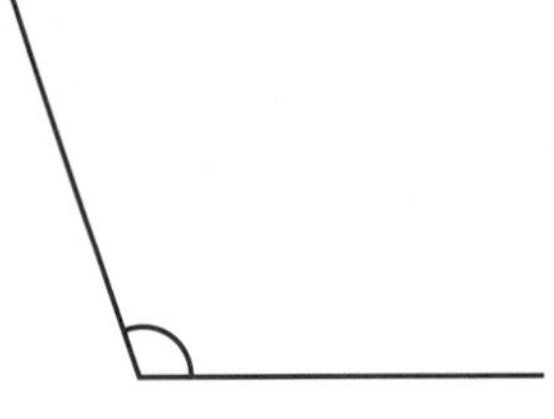

Estimate ________

Measurement ________

f.

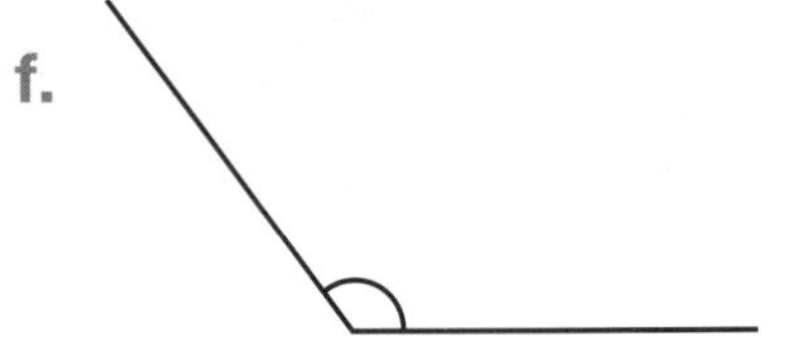

Estimate ________

Measurement ________

2. Now draw these angles, using a protractor to measure accurately.

a. 69° angle

b. 101° angle

c. 88° angle

Angle facts

Make sure you are aware of the different angle names and what they mean: right, acute, obtuse, reflex. Remember that a right angle = 90°, a straight line = 180° and a complete turn = 360°.

1. Name the following angles. Choose from the names given below.

reflex angle * right angle * acute angle * obtuse angle

a.

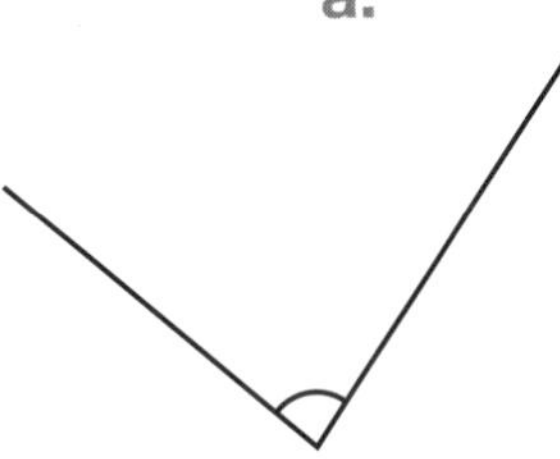

____

b.

____

c.

____

d.

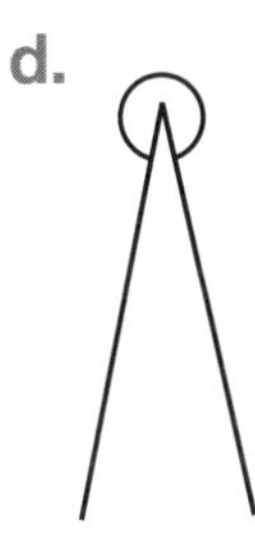

____

2. Calculate the following angles marked with the letter a.

a.

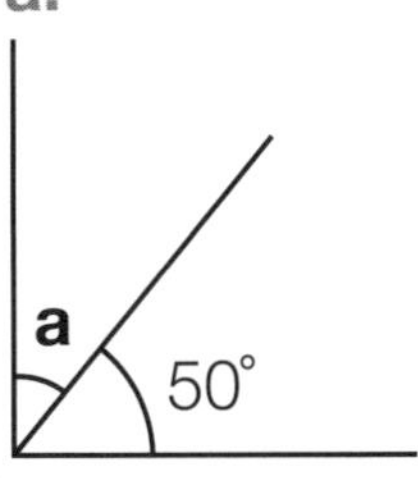

a = __________

b.

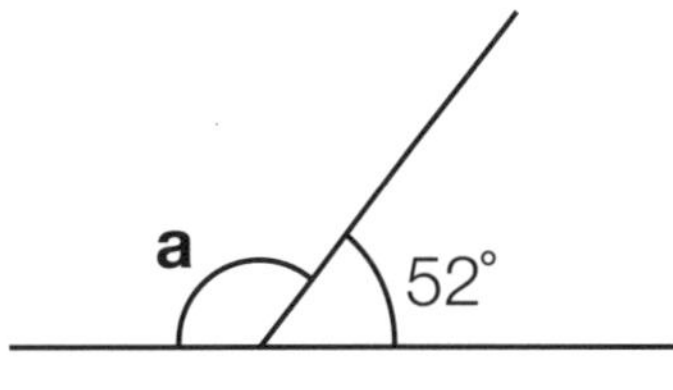

a = __________

c.

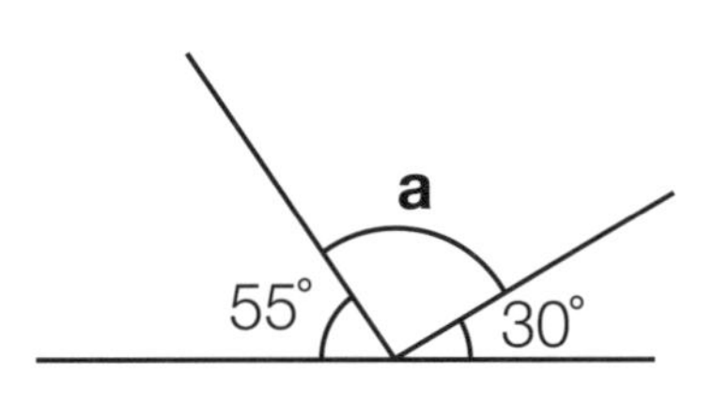

a = __________

d.

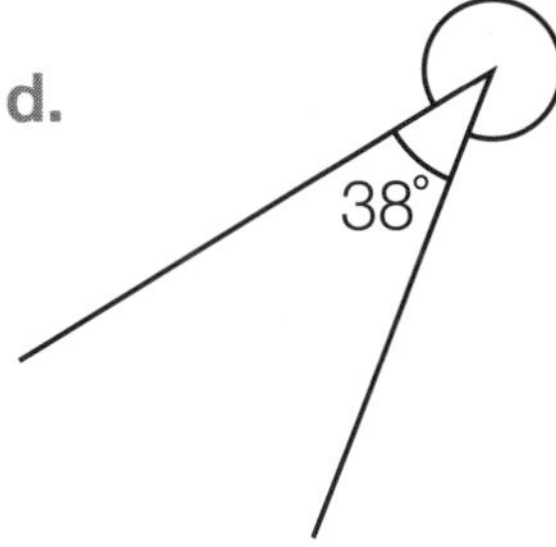

a = __________

e.

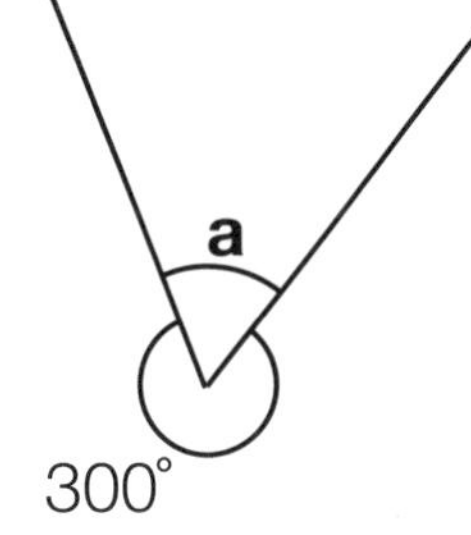

a = __________

f.

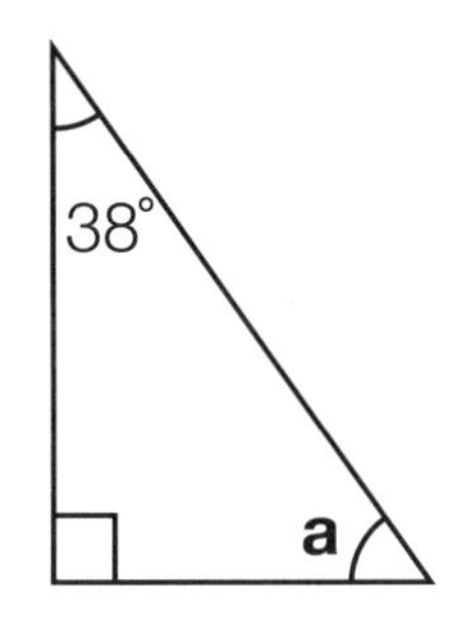

a = __________

Identifying 2D shapes

It is important to know the names given to common 2D shapes and how to recognise them according to their properties. When talking about 2D shapes, 'regular' means that all the sides and angles will be identical, while irregular means that some sides and angles will be different.

1. Read each description carefully. Identify the shape and then draw it.

a. A regular quadrilateral. ____________________	**b.** A parallelogram with four equal sides and equal opposite angles. ____________________
c. A triangle with no equal angles or sides. ____________________	**d.** A shape with three sets of parallel sides. ____________________
e. A shape with eight sides where no sides or angles are the same size. ____________________	**f.** Describe and name these shapes. A B **A** ____________________ ____________________ **B** ____________________ ____________________

2D shape problems

Use a protractor so that the right angle between the two short sides of each triangle is constructed accurately.

Square the two sides of the triangles given and add them together. What relationship do they have with the square of the third and longest side? $3^2 + 4^2 = 9 + 16 = ?$

1. Penny says that pentagons don't contain any right angles. Draw a pentagon that contains three right angles to prove her wrong!

2. Construct right-angled triangles with these pairs of short sides.

3cm and 4cm   2cm and 2.5cm   4cm and 6cm

3. For each triangle, measure accurately the length of the longest side. What do you notice?

____

4. Measure the angles of each triangle. What do you notice?

____

In the net

The net of a 3D shape is the flat shape that can be folded and stuck together to make the 3D shape. Take some clean food boxes apart to see what their nets look like. It will help to look at fully-made-up versions of the shapes before attempting to draw out their nets.

1. Kate is having a little trouble drawing the nets of solid shapes. Help her to complete the net for a cube and a triangular prism.

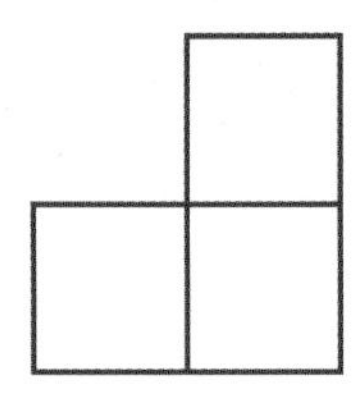

2. Here is the net for a cuboid.
Robert wants to cut it out and stick it together.
Draw the minimum number of flaps required so that each edge is securely fastened.

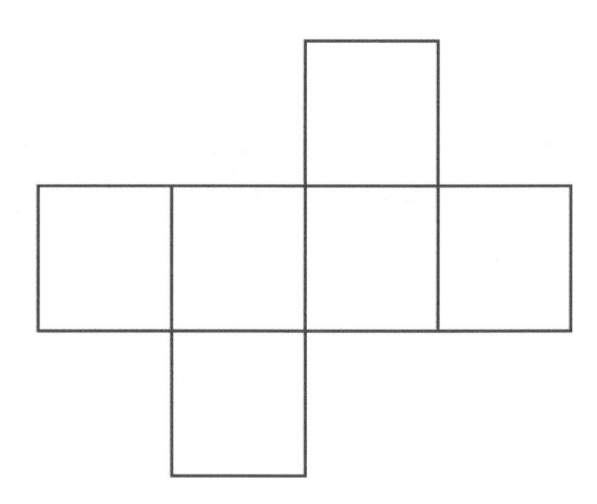

3. In this space, draw the net of a square-based pyramid. Use a set-square to draw the base, which must measure 2cm × 2cm.

3D shape sorting

Make sure you understand the words 'parallel' and 'perpendicular'. Parallel lines or faces are the same distance apart from each other all the way along their length. Perpendicular lines or faces are those that meet each other at right angles.

Answer these questions about the properties of 3D solids. Think carefully about the 3D solids that you know and recall their properties.

1. How many pairs of parallel faces does a cube have? ____________________

2. How many pairs of parallel edges does a square-based pyramid have? ____________

3. Which solids have no perpendicular faces?

   ____

4. Which solid has only two edges? ____________________

5. Which solid has six vertices?____________________

6. Look at all the shapes mentioned in the questions and answers above. Choose some sorting criteria and label your Venn diagram. Write the names on the shapes onto the Venn diagram.

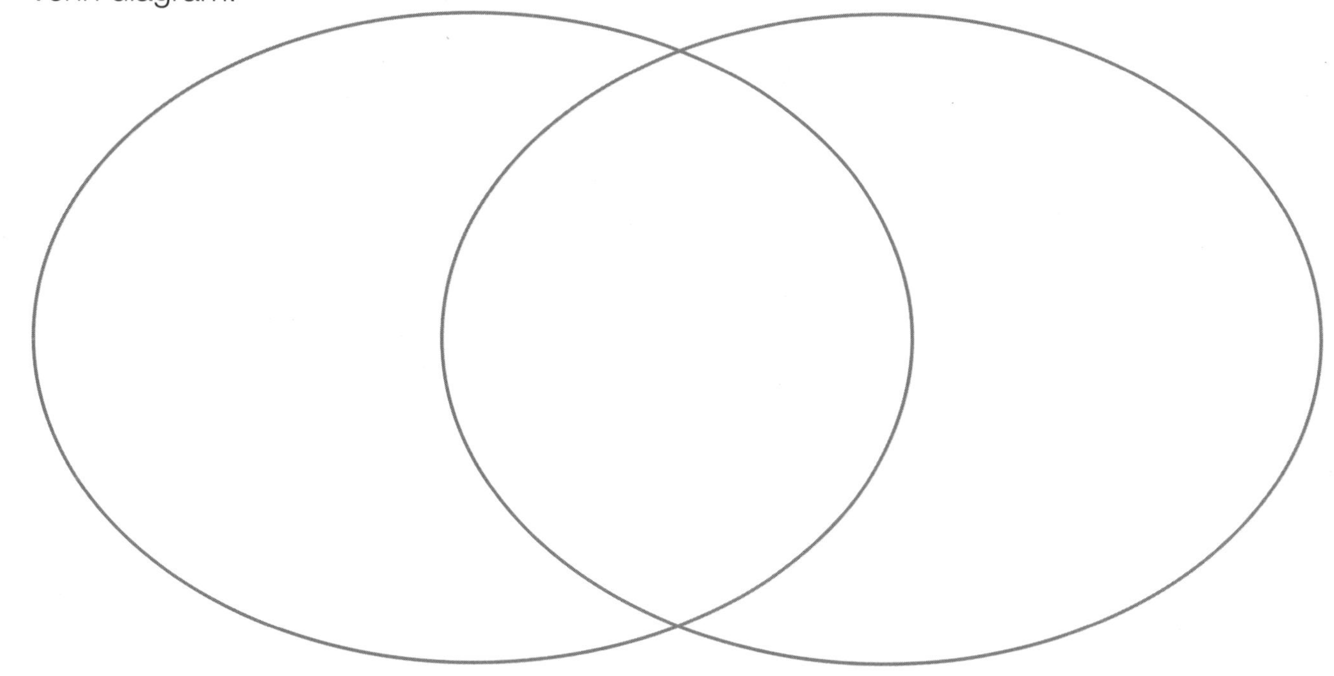

Picture coordinates

Coordinates give accurate positions on the grid. They are worked out by reading the horizontal axis first (across) and then the vertical axis (up or down). Make sure coordinates are written in the correct style, for example (–3, 2).

Design a coordinate picture for a friend to try.

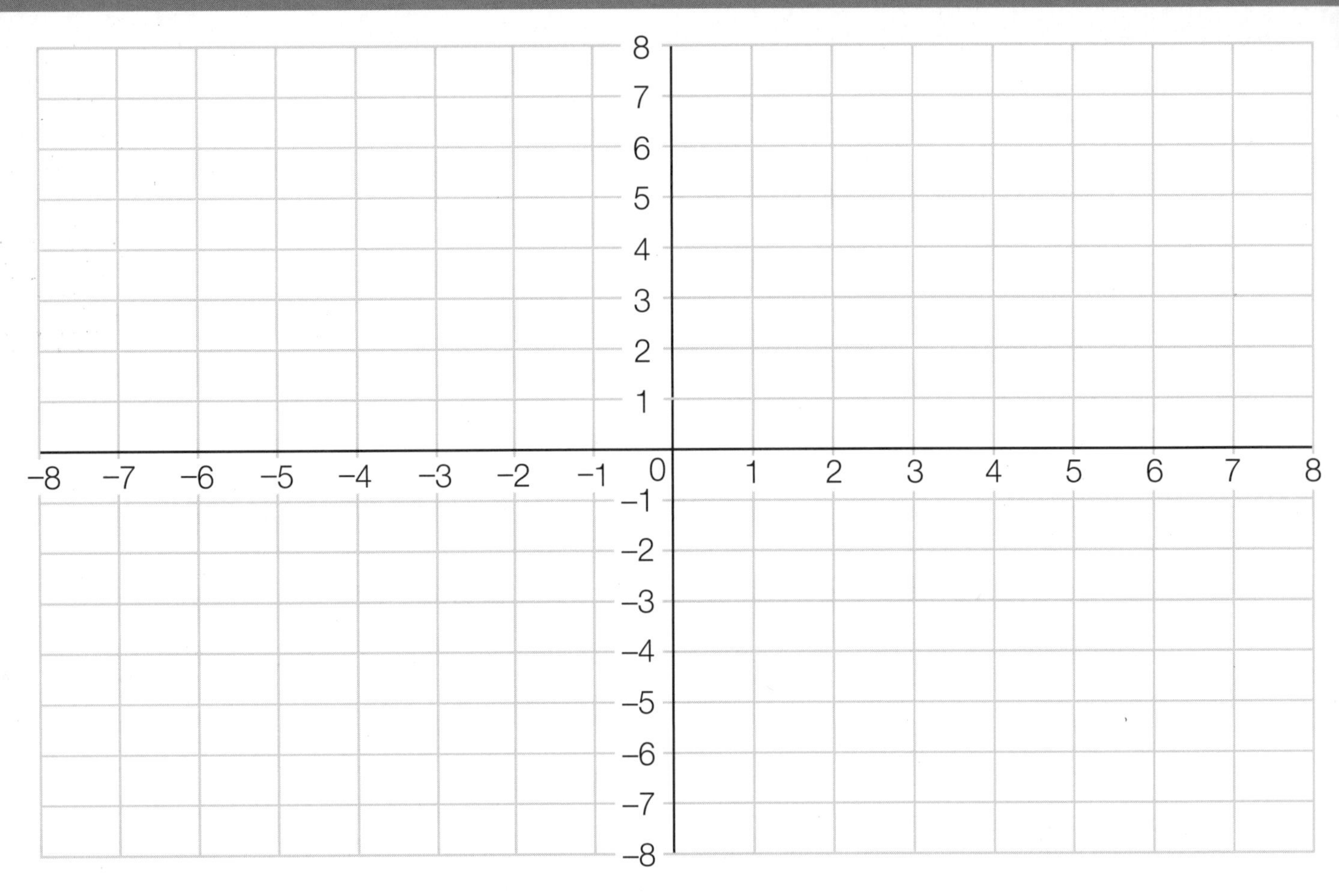

1. Use the grid above to plan your design. Your design must go into all four quadrants.
2. Write down the coordinates of your design and give them to your partner to copy onto a blank coordinate grid. Don't let your partner see your picture until they have finished. Were your coordinates accurate? How careful were they in following your instructions?

   Points to remember:

   - The design must be composed of straight lines.
   - The coordinates must be written in order, so that your partner can join them up.
   - You may have more than one set of coordinates, so that it is possible to have smaller shapes inside a larger one (for example, an eye).

Translate and reflect

Sometimes it will be necessary to read and plot coordinates in all four quadrants. Remember, across coordinates must be read first. Make sure the minus signs are shown clearly when you use coordinates that include them.

1. **Draw a suitable regular or irregular shape in the top left-hand quadrant. Label its coordinates.**
2. **Translate the shape once and draw the new shape on the grid. Make a note of the translation, for example 8 right and 3 up, and label the coordinates of the new shape.**

Translation: ______________________________

3. **Reflect the same shape in the vertical and horizontal axes, making sure the coordinates are correct each time. Label the coordinates of each reflection.**

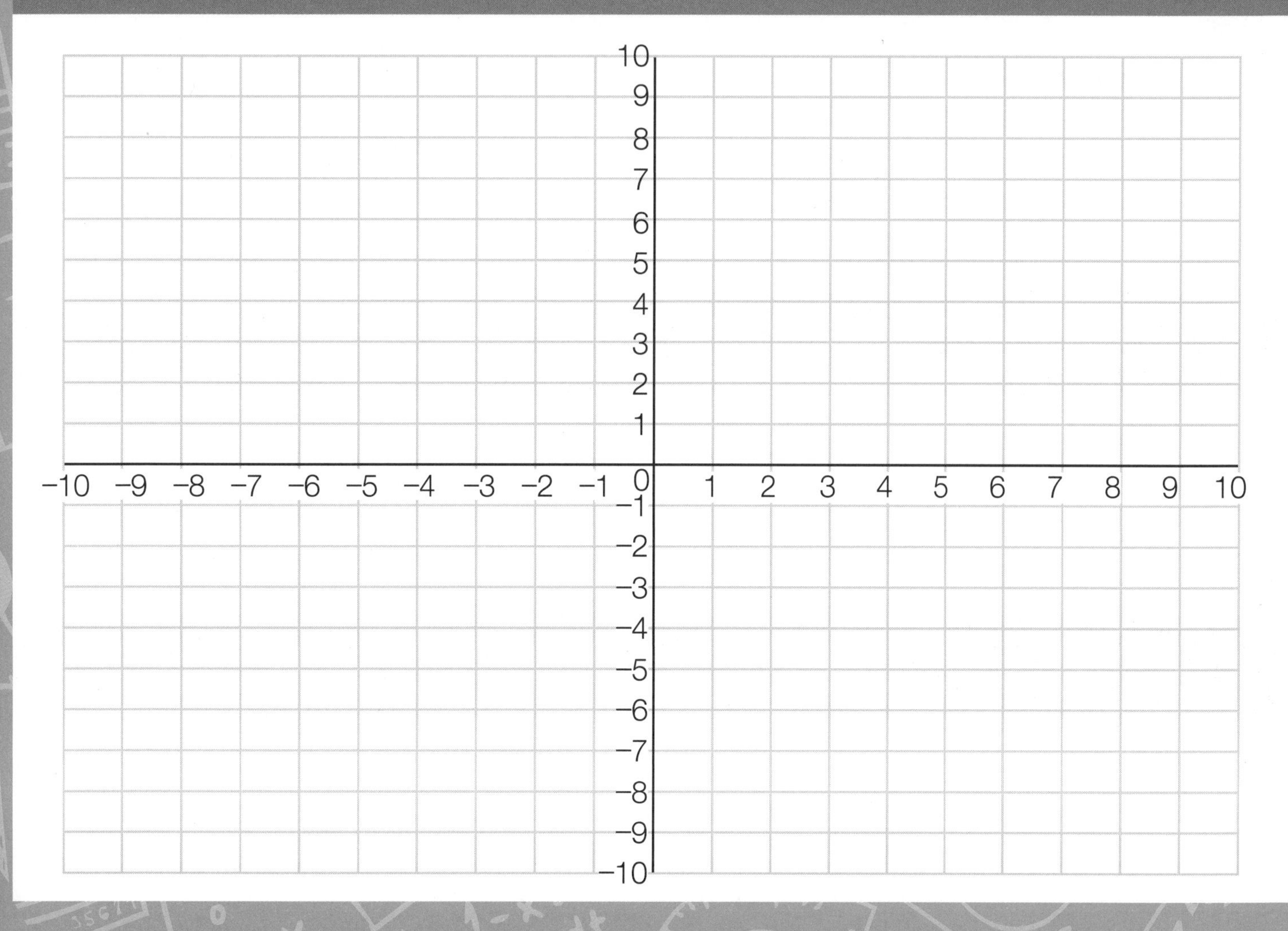

Winning teams' pie chart

Pie charts are divided into sectors. The largest sector shows the item with the highest frequency and the smallest sector show the one with the lowest frequency.

These pie charts show the results of hockey games played by two schools. Southwick School have played 20 matches, while Northport School have played 28 matches.

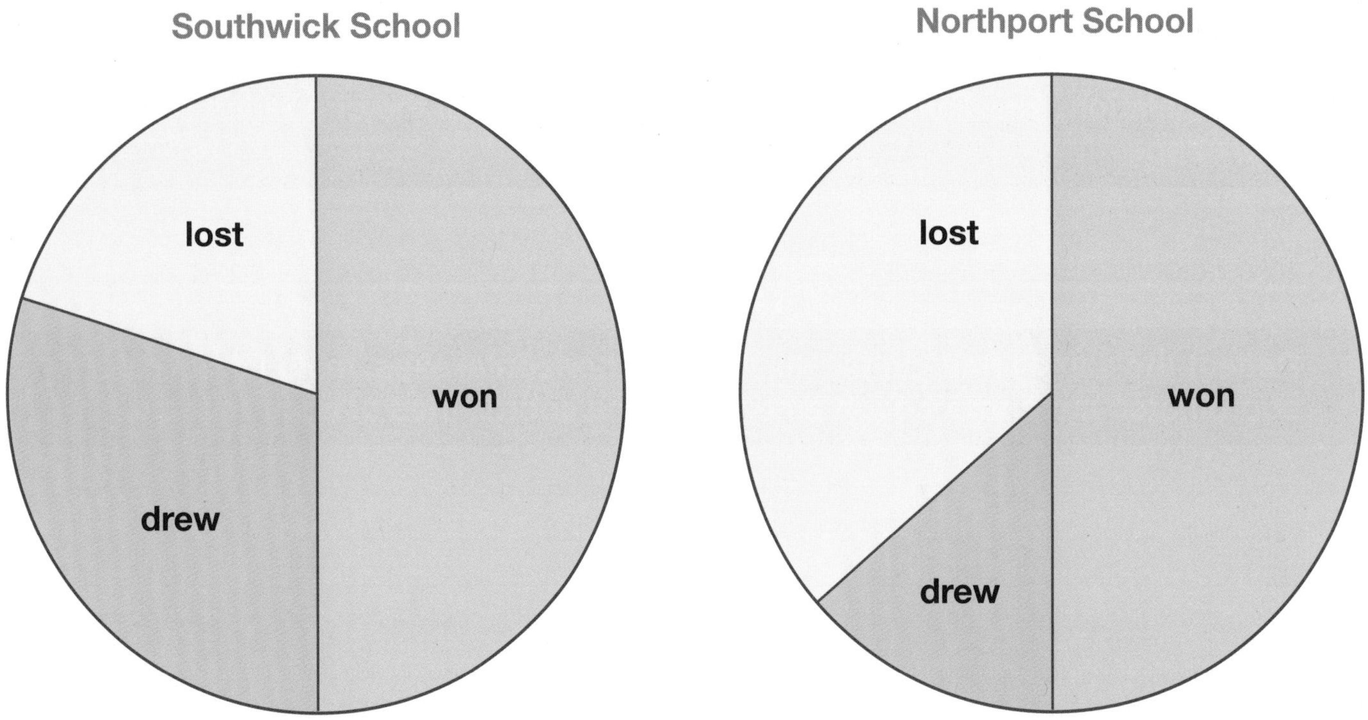

1. As accurately as possible, say how many games you think each school won, drew and lost. You can divide each circle into quarters if it will help.

Southwick School: Won ____________ Drew ____________ Lost ____________

Northport School: Won ____________ Drew ____________ Lost ____________

2. Angela said: "Half of each pie chart shows 'won', so the two teams must have won the same number of games." Is she correct? Explain how you know.

____

____

My day

Some rounding of times will be necessary to make angle calculations easier. Times must total 24 hours (100%) and the whole circle must be used. Angles should be measured from the centre of the circle, where a complete turn is equal to 360 degrees.

You are going to draw a pie chart to show how you spend your time in a typical day at the weekend.

1. Think about how you spend your day (24 hours) and put the information into this chart (for example, sleeping = 8 hours and 30 minutes). Round up or down to the nearest 30 minutes.

Activity	Hours and minutes

2. Draw a pie chart to show proportionately how your time is spent.
3. Write the percentage of the day spent doing each activity in the relevant section.

Interpret a line graph

A line graph is able to show and compare two sets of information. It is useful for comparing two sets of information over a period of time.

This line graph shows the votes cast for the Red Party and the Blue Party in the last six elections. The points have been joined in each case to show trends over a period of time.

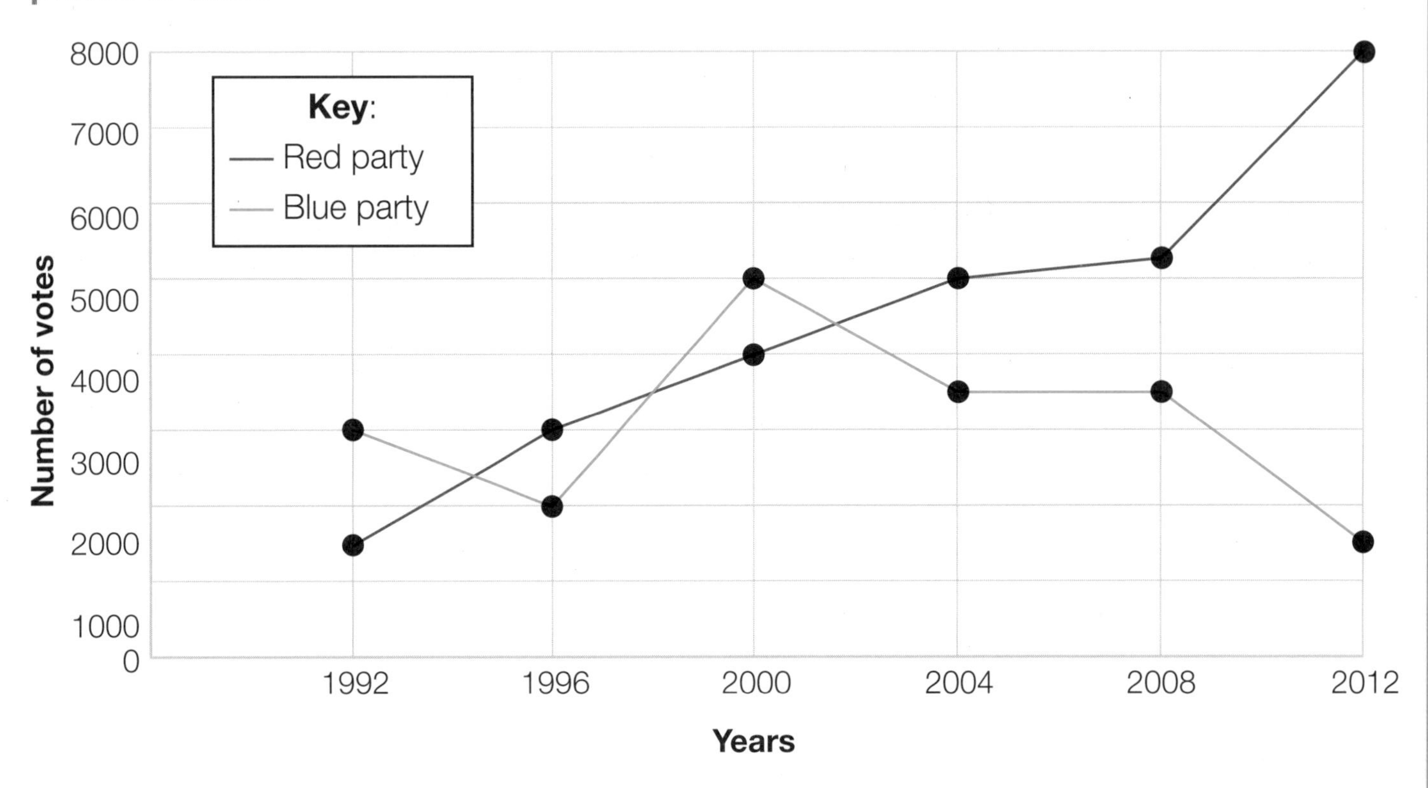

1. Give the highest and lowest vote for both parties. ____________________

2. How many votes in total did the Red Party get in 2000 and 2004? ____________________

3. How many votes in total did the Blue Party get in 2008 and 2012? ____________________

4. In which years did the Blue Party achieve the same number of votes? ____________________

5. In which years did the Blue Party do better than the Red Party? ____________________

6. Which party has grown steadily in popularity? ____________________

7. Describe the performance of the Red Party in the twenty-year period of the elections.

____

Construct a line graph

The information in the box shows the sales figures of the Delight Chocolate Company's top two bars, Whizzo and Crumble, during the first six months of the year.

Month	Whizzo	Crumble
January	300	200
February	450	100
March	500	250
April	200	50
May	600	350
June	800	750

1. Make a line graph to show the information for both chocolate bars. Decide what should be shown on each axis, what scale should be used, and how points should be marked and joined up. Remember to include a key.

2. Analyse the information shown on the graph by making up three questions. These might include: Which brand has the better sales figures? Which was the worst month for sales?

____

____

____

Mean rainfall

Remember that there are different kinds of averages.

- Range: the difference between the smallest and largest numbers in the group.
- Mode: the item that occurs most in a list.
- Mean: the average found by adding all the numbers and dividing by the number of items.

This bar chart shows the amount of rainfall on the holiday island Paradisio.

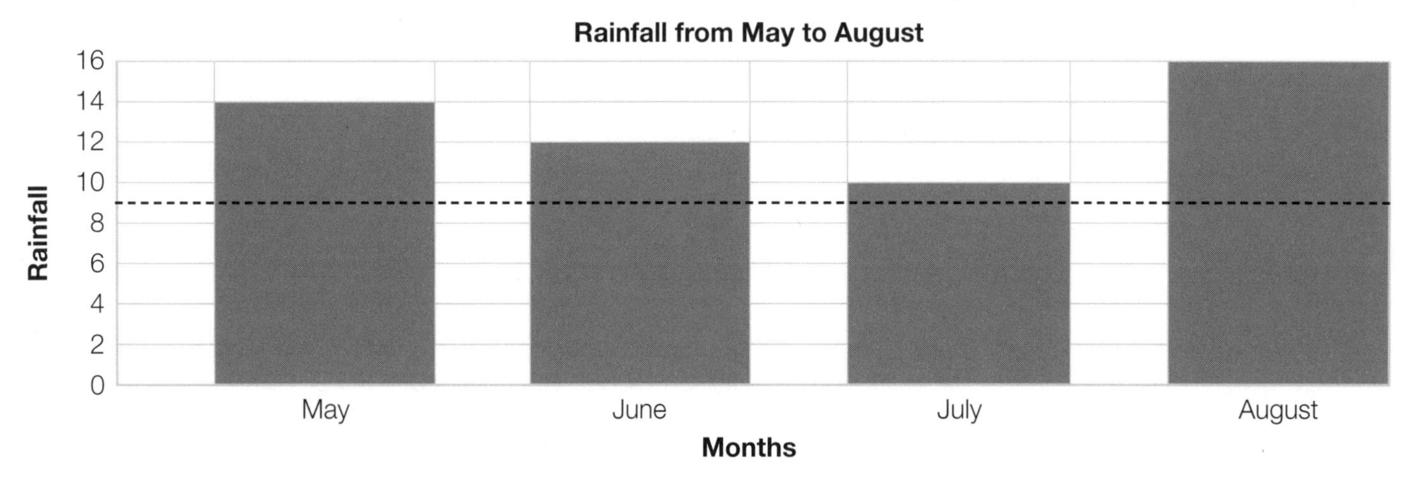

1. Justine says: "The dotted line on the chart shows the mean rainfall for the four months." Use the chart to explain why Justine cannot be correct.

   Justine is incorrect because ______________________________

   ____

2. What is the mean rainfall on Island Paradisio for the four months?

   ____

3. Give different values for the monthly rainfall totals but keep the mean the same.

   ____

4. What is the range of rainfall in these four months? ______________________________

   ____

5. Write a number in each of these boxes so that the mode of the five numbers is 11.

Mean temperatures

The mean is found by adding all the numbers in a list together and dividing by the number of amounts. The median is the middle number in a set of values. You will need to arrange the values in order first, smallest to largest to find the median.

These are the temperatures (in °C) for a two-week period on the holiday island Paradisio.

Week 1	25, 26, 26, 23, 24, 30, 28
Week 2	28, 28, 32, 28, 33, 35, 26
Week 3	23, 19, 18, 15, 24, 21, 27
Week 4	25, 21, 24, 31, 29, 19, 28

1. Find the mean and the median temperature for each of the four weeks.

Week 1: Median ______________________ Mean ______________________

Week 2: Median ______________________ Mean ______________________

Week 3: Median ______________________ Mean ______________________

Week 4: Median ______________________ Mean ______________________

Progress chart

Making progress? Tick (✔) the cogs as you complete each section of the book.

	Most questions completed	All questions completed
Number and place value	⚙	⚙
More practice?		
Calculation	⚙	⚙
More practice?		
Fractions, decimals and percentages	⚙	⚙
More practice?		
Ratio and proportion	⚙	⚙
More practice?		
Algebra	⚙	⚙
More practice?		
Measurement	⚙	⚙
More practice?		
Geometry: properties of shapes	⚙	⚙
More practice?		
Geometry: position and direction	⚙	⚙
More practice?		
Statistics	⚙	⚙
More practice?		

WELL DONE!

YOU DID IT!

Name: ______________________

You have completed

YEAR 6 MATHS

Practice Book

Age: ____________ Date: ____________

Index